CARMELITE BIBLE MEDITATIO

LET IT BE

Praying the Scriptures in compan
Mary, the Mother of Jesus

BY JOSEPH CHALMERS, O.CARM.

LET IT BE

*Praying the Scriptures in company with
Mary, the Mother of Jesus*

BY JOSEPH CHALMERS, O.CARM.

WITH A FOREWORD BY NICHOLAS KING, S.J.

Saint Albert's Press & Edizioni Carmelitane
2010

EDIZIONI
CARMELITANE

First published 2010 by Saint Albert's Press & Edizioni Carmelitane.

Saint Albert's Press
Whitefriars, 35 Tanners Street,
Faversham, Kent, ME13 7JN, United Kingdom
www.carmelite.org
ISBN-10: 0-904849-41-4
ISBN-13: 978-0-904849-41-7

Edizioni Carmelitane
Centro Internationale S. Alberto
Via Sforza Pallavicini, 10
00193 Roma, Italy
www.carmelites.info/edizioni
ISBN-13: 978-88-7288-116-3

Edited and designed by Johan Bergström-Allen, Carmelite Projects & Publications Office, York.

Typeset by Ing. Jakub Kubů, Prague, Czech Republic
Printed by ERMAT Praha s.r.o., Czech Republic.
Production coordinated by Pavel Kindermann on behalf of Karmelitánské nakladatelství s.r.o., Kostelní Vydří 58, 380 01 Dačice, Czech Republic, www.kna.cz.

Saint Albert's Press would like to thank the communities, churches, libraries, galleries and individuals who have supplied artwork for this book, all of which is linked in one way or another to the Carmelite tradition of devotion to Mary. Saint Albert's Press would like to thank the various photographers whose work is reproduced in this book, including: Johan Bergström-Allen, T.O.C.; Richard Copsey, O.Carm.; Antony Lester, O.Carm.; Ruth Long; Kevin Melody, O.Carm.; Riccardo Palazzi, O.Carm.; James Postlethwaite. The cover image is of Mary as 'Flos Carmeli' (Flower of Carmel), by Moira Forsyth, at Aylesford Carmelite Priory in Kent, England.

The British Province of Carmelites would like to express its thanks to those who have given their generous endorsement and encouragement to the publication of this book, including: His Eminence Cardinal Keith Patrick O'Brien, Archbishop of St Andrews and Edinburgh; Rt. Rev. Malcolm McMahon, O.P., Bishop of Nottingham; Fr. Nicholas King, S.J., Chair of the Catholic Biblical Association of Great Britain.

CONTENTS

FOREWORD

It is a very great pleasure to welcome this enchanting and timely book. It is enchanting because it speaks of prayer from the inside; the author, a former Prior General of the Carmelites, has clearly "been there, done that". It is timely, first, because we live in a day when Catholics are sometimes a bit embarrassed by our devotion to Our Lady; our Protestant friends may chide us that it is not really biblical. The second reason is that Catholics are sometimes a bit nervous about the Bible, fearing that scholars have perhaps shown that the whole Bible is "all a pack of lies". They haven't, of course, but that is what people sometimes find themselves thinking.

This is a book from someone who is clearly at home in the academic study of the Bible, but also for whom *Lectio Divina* is a familiar way of praying, as he takes all the New Testament texts about Mary and invites us to read them, reflect on them, respond to them, rest in them (a delightful touch, this), and, finally, act upon them. This *Lectio Divina* is once more coming alive in our age, as Catholics rediscover the Bible at the heart of our life of prayer. In this book the effect of this approach to prayer is to make Mary's story into our story; the author allows the reader to develop his or her prayer in dialogue with God by putting some excellent questions at the end of each reflection. For that is the aim of it all, to enable us to follow our human vocation to "become God", as the author is not afraid to put it.

What is particularly helpful is the way Fr. Joseph uses many different English translations of the texts that he puts before us, and gives useful notes on each biblical author, to place them in their context. He is not afraid of looking at the "difficult" passages, such as the mention of Jesus' brothers in *Mark* 6, or the mistaken date of the census in *Luke* 2, and putting various possible interpretations before us. As befits a Carmelite, there is a great deal here on John of the Cross, that great store of wisdom on the life of prayer.

The book is also beautifully illustrated, and that will help you to pray your way through it. It is a book not to read so much as to *do*, and I warmly commend it to the reader. It is a worthy successor to the author's excellent meditations on the texts about Elijah, *The Sound of Silence*.

Nicholas King, S.J.
Campion Hall, Oxford
Chair of the Catholic Biblical Association of Great Britain

INTRODUCTION

This book is a collection of all the New Testament texts that mention Mary, the mother of Jesus in some way. The approach taken is not an academic study, although I have included some of the insights from the more recent New Testament studies (a select bibliography is given at the end of the book). This book follows the movement of *Lectio Divina*, the ancient way of prayer based on reading the Word of God and opening us to intimacy with God. It is important to be guided in some way when reading Scripture so that we can be as open as possible to what God is saying to us and not let our own prejudices blind us to the truth. I have been guided by the studies mentioned in the select bibliography as well as others. I was inspired to write this present book when I translated into English a brief but profound work by Klemens Stock, S.J.[1] He studies each text and then tries to paint a composite picture of Mary from all the data that the New Testament gives us. It is this approach to praying with Scripture that I adopted with my previous book, *The Sound of Silence*, which reflected on all the Bible passages relating to the prophet Elijah who, like Mary, is so important for the Carmelite Order's self-understanding.

It is important to read each text as we have it in the New Testament, rather than what we think it should say, because God has something to say to us in the actual text. The Bible is like a whole library, and in a library there are many different kinds of books: history, fiction, poetry, love stories, and so on. You can find all this and more in the Bible. Fundamentally the Bible is a story about God's dealings with humanity and this story is told in many different ways. God chose one nation out of all the peoples of the Earth, and this nation was to be a light for the world (*Isaiah* 42:6; 49:6). The New Testament is part two of this story. God has loved the world so much that God sent His Son not to condemn the world but so that we might have life in abundance (cf. *John* 3:17).

It might seem obvious to say that the New Testament is about Jesus Christ. He is the final and full revelation of God and goes beyond anything we could have expected or hoped for. The focus of the Christian faith must be on Jesus Christ and it is principally through the Word of God that we can know him. Why then write about Mary, the mother of Jesus? The characters that appear in the New Testament are important only insofar as they relate to Jesus and tell us something about him and about God's plan of salvation for humanity. It seems clear that Mary's role as the mother of Jesus is more than peripheral. She

---

1   Klemens Stock, *Mary the Mother of the Lord in the New Testament*, (Rome: Edizioni Carmelitane, 2006).

received a unique vocation from God, and her response to the call from God and to her Son can instruct us as to how we might respond to our own vocation.

Some people have difficulty with the New Testament as, despite the large areas of agreement among the Gospels and letters, there are also some disagreements. How many miracles of the feeding of the multitude were there? How many women went to the tomb on the morning of the resurrection? Which genealogy of Jesus is correct? Why do only two Gospels tells us about the birth of Jesus? There are many other interesting questions that scholars of the Bible love to debate. However it should not surprise us that there are different approaches to the story of Jesus. No two witnesses tell exactly the same story about what they have seen. Everyone filters their experience through their own personality. Far from detracting from the richness of the Christian story, it adds to it.

There is no complete agreement about how exactly each piece of the New Testament came to be written. Different oral traditions grew up depending on who first preached the Good News and to whom it was addressed. These traditions told the story of Jesus from different perspectives and they all help us to understand who is Jesus Christ and what is his significance for our lives. The biblical writers did not have our questions and our preoccupations in mind; they had their own issues. Scripture is indeed the Word of God but this Word comes to us through the words and thought-patterns of human beings. These human beings were shaped largely by their own culture. The faith of the Christian Church is that Jesus Christ is God Incarnate. This means that God has entered fully into our human story and it is from within this story that we meet our God. This can lead to some frustration at times when we have to struggle to understand what it is that God is really saying to us. In order to grasp what a piece of Scripture means, we have to try to understand a little bit about the world in which the original writer lived.

The Gospels are not straight history. How they came to be in the form that we have them is complex. The evangelists and the other New Testament writers too, used various traditions, some of which had been passed on by word of mouth while others were written down. What the New Testament writers chose to write was shaped by the concerns and experiences of the communities in which they lived. They seemed to feel much freer than a modern author would about using sources. Therefore, while there is a considerable degree of agreement on some issues, there is also a lot of disagreement, and this will become apparent as we go through the different New Testament texts concerning the figure of Mary, the mother of Jesus.

Should the differences among New Testament writers disturb us? No, because their different interpretations add to the richness of the whole picture. Different witnesses to any event will remember different aspects even though they may agree on the central core. If four people witness a woman's hat being blown off in the wind, there will be four different accounts of the colour of the hat. The woman herself will be described differently; perhaps the witnesses may even give different times for this momentous event. Certainly the woman herself will give a totally different account. However, from all this information can be gleaned the nucleus of what actually happened. What is important in the story is that the woman's hat was blown off in the wind.

The Gospels do not answer our modern question: "Did this really happen exactly as you described it?" What the Gospels are trying to do is to get at the meaning of the life, mission, death and resurrection of Jesus. The Gospel-writers tell stories about Jesus and recount things that he said to illustrate particular points that are important to them. One writer will include something and one will leave it out; one will change a story to make a point in a clearer way. There are about 2,000 years separating us from the New Testament, and it can be frustrating that it does not always answer the questions we have. However, the whole Bible is a message from God. If we only want our modern questions answered, we could miss what God is saying to us. Therefore we need to read the Scriptures with great respect and allow the Word of God to take up home in our hearts. Taken altogether, the various kinds of writings that make up the New Testament give us good news about God's intervention in human history in a definitive way and they call each one of us to faith in Jesus the Christ, who reveals the face of God in a unique way. Mary, the mother of the Lord, had to struggle to accept what God was saying to her and to respond in faith to her son. She "pondered all these things in her heart" (*Luke* 2:51). As you pray the various texts that speak of her, may you glorify the Lord along with her (cf. *Luke* 1:46).

Structure of the Book

This book is divided into sections, and each section treats of the larger context from which comes the particular texts we will be examining. Usually we hear or read only a small portion of the Scriptures at a time, and it is important to have this wider context in mind when we approach each text. Within the section there are several reflections in which the movement of *Lectio Divina* is used to draw out the implications of each text.

Lectio Divina is an ancient way of prayer that has become popular again in recent years.[2] Originally it was used by monks and hermits in the desert to allow the Word of God to produce the fruit of contemplation within them. Contemplation is intimacy with God, which itself bears abundant fruit in our lives. It is a gift of God that we cannot produce or merit by ourselves. However, we can open ourselves to receive this gift when and if God wishes to give it to us. *Lectio Divina* remains a personal way of prayer but it can also very fruitfully be used by groups.

When we go to pray it is important that we remember who is the partner in this dialogue. We are going to enter into a dialogue with God, and therefore each reflection begins with a short prayer that we might be open to what God wants to say to us through the particular piece of Scripture before us. The opening prayer is only a suggestion. Perhaps a prayer in your own words would be better.

Then there is the actual Bible text. Throughout this book I have varied the translation of the Bible from where I have taken the text. The original language of the New Testament was, of course, Greek. That was not the first language of many of the New Testament writers, but it was a sort of international language, much like English in our days. There are many different English translations of the Bible today. I give some description of the particular translation used in each reflection. The older ones are obviously written in a rather archaic style and it will be interesting to see whether the more modern translations make things clearer, or whether they lose something important. It can be useful to compare different translations from time to time as it can help us to understand a particular text to see it from two different perspectives. Usually the words are a little different though the meaning is clearly the same. However, from time to time a particular translation can in fact change the clear meaning. You may prefer to use a version of the Bible with which you are more at home. Just be aware that no translation is perfect; each has its good points and its defects.

Following the Bible text itself there is a section entitled "READ". Here I try to give some indications as to what the writer originally intended. Countless volumes have been written by biblical scholars in which each line and word is studied from every possible angle. Here I have used some of these studies to give a brief outline of what the general consensus has to say about each text.

---

2   There are very many books about the theory and history of *Lectio Divina*. Two of the best introductions in English are: Thelma Hall, *Too Deep For Words* (New York: Paulist Press, 1988); and Michael Casey, *Sacred Reading* (Liguori, Missouri: Triumph Books, 1996).

The part entitled "REFLECT" is intended to personalise the Word of God. What might God be saying to me, or to each member of a group? I have provided questions to help this process.

"RESPOND" is the traditional moment when we speak to God from the heart. I have indicated a prayer, either from Scripture or Christian Tradition, that might be of help on this step. Of course it is intended to lead to a personal response to God, and no one can complete this step for you.

The section entitled "REST" is a step in *Lectio Divina* that traditionally was called "contemplation". This word has a long tradition and has often been misunderstood as something esoteric, but in essence it is entirely simple. After all our effort we are invited to simply rest in the Word of God. We let go of our own words, thoughts and prayers, so that we can be still and know that God is God (cf. *Psalm* 46:11). What happens then is for God to decide.

The final movement is "ACT", by means of which we try to bring the insights that we have received during our prayer into our daily life, so that slowly but surely we may open our existence to the transformative power of God.

The different steps are not intended to be rigorously followed. It is important to go where you believe God is leading you, even if that means skipping over one or two of the steps. Perhaps we might also be led back to the beginning again or invited to remain at a particular point for a while longer. Saint Paul wrote to the Church in Galatia: "For freedom Christ has set you free" (*Galatians* 5:1). Use this book in whatever way you feel drawn.

The final reflection is the application of the method of *Lectio Divina* to a short excerpt from a Church document on the role of Mary, the mother of the Lord, in our lives.

The writing of the Word of God.
Window by George Walsh in the Chapel of Avila Discalced Carmelite Friary, Dublin.

Mary in the Gospel of Matthew

The Evangelist Matthew depicted as a winged man or angel.
Ceramic by Adam Kossowski in St. Joseph's Chapel, Aylesford Priory, Kent, England.

Matthew's Gospel was always placed first in the list of New Testament writings, and it was the most quoted by the early Church Fathers. It was believed to have been written first, and by one of Jesus' own specially chosen apostles. These claims have been challenged for many years and there are various theories regarding which was the first gospel to be written, and who actually wrote each one. We do not need to go into these difficult questions here, but it is important to know that the Matthew's Gospel we have today, though it may be traced back to very early traditions, is unlikely to have been written directly by one of the original twelve apostles of Jesus. It is likely that before any of the Gospels were written that some sort of compilation of the sayings of Jesus, and perhaps also of his miracles, existed. Certainly stories about Jesus were passed on by word of mouth. Matthew (or whoever actually compiled the Gospel we traditionally attach to his name) seems to have written his version after Mark's Gospel, and used a lot of the material found there. Matthew's Gospel was probably written around the year 90 A.D., that is, about 60 years after the passion, death and resurrection of Jesus. Like the whole of the New Testament, Matthew's Gospel is written from the perspective of the earth-shattering event of the resurrection of Jesus from the dead. This means that the Gospel writers sometimes inserted fully developed Christian faith into stories before the death and resurrection of Jesus.

Like all New Testament documents, Matthew's Gospel was written within a particular community and for a particular community. Therefore, what a specific text meant for the original people for whom it was written is important, and this must be the basis for what it might mean for us. Otherwise we will make the Bible mean what we want it to mean, rather than listening to what God is saying to us through the written word.

Matthew's community seems to have been principally made up of people who knew Judaism intimately and this fact determined his basic approach to the telling of the story of Jesus. Indeed Matthew does not consider Christianity to be a separate religion to Judaism. He presents the one people of God, made up of Jew and Gentile, all who have come to believe that Jesus is the Messiah sent by God. Jesus is of course the main character of Matthew's Gospel, and God is the prime mover in the story. Jesus' birth, mission, passion, death and resurrection all occur according to God's will. God is in control of the flow of history from creation till the final judgement when Christ will come again to judge the living and the dead. The central symbol in the preaching of Jesus is "the kingdom of heaven", which is Matthew's way of describing the reign of God over all human beings and over all creation, visible and invisible. This is present here and now, despite those who oppose God, and despite appearances, and will be fully revealed at the end of time. What dominates the Gospel is the struggle between the two kingdoms: the kingdom of heaven and the kingdom of this world.

The name of "Mary" occurs five times in relation to the mother of Jesus in Matthew's Gospel (1:16, 20; 2:11; 13:55). Nine times she is named simply "mother" (1:18; 2:11, 13, 14, 20, 21; 12:46, 47; 13:55). Matthew's image of Mary is the one whom God called to be the virgin mother of Christ who is the saviour of Israel and the whole of humanity. Through the divine creative power, God made Mary capable of bearing Jesus without a human father. Matthew never mentions what Mary thought, felt or said. Her personal experience is excluded from his account. She is completely dedicated to her vocation as the mother of the saviour, and in this way she performs an unrepeatable role in the history of salvation.

*This Black Madonna was carved from a piece of Irish bog oak by Clare Sheridan
(a cousin of Winston Churchill) who lived at Allington Castle
in the English county of Kent in the 1950s when it housed a Carmelite community.
The folds of the wood have been used to form the folds of the dress.*

MARY IN THE GENEALOGY OF JESUS

Matthew 1:1-16

Opening Prayer

Gracious and loving God, thank you for the gift of life that has been mediated through so many ancestors. Thank you for sending Christ your Son, as our long awaited saviour. He took flesh in the womb of the Virgin Mary and entered our human story through her. Help me to enter into the mystery of her virginal motherhood so that I may receive the blessings you want to give me through her.

Text

Read attentively the following Bible text for the first time in order to get an idea of the overall sense and to take in the details. I have used the translation from the *New Revised Standard Version*.[3] This is a revision from the *Revised Standard Version* dating from 1952. It modernises and simplifies the language of the *RSV*, and also revises it to make the language inclusive. You will note that in the first and sixteenth verses, the word "Messiah" is used instead of "Christ". We are used to using the name "Christ" almost like a surname, but in fact it is a title, which translates the Hebrew word for the one whom the people were awaiting as the saviour or Messiah. Since Matthew's Gospel was originally intended for people who knew the Bible well, it was important to show that Jesus had fulfilled the promises made by God and that he was in fact the Messiah.

> [1] An account of the genealogy of Jesus the Messiah, the son of David, the son of Abraham. [2] Abraham was the father of Isaac, and Isaac the father of Jacob, and Jacob the father of Judah and his brothers, [3] and Judah the father of Perez and Zerah by Tamar, and Perez the father of Hezron, and Hezron the father of Aram, [4] and Aram the father of Aminadab, and Aminadab the father of Nahshon, and Nahshon the father of Salmon, [5] and Salmon the father of Boaz by Rahab, and Boaz the father of Obed by Ruth,

---

3   *The New Revised Standard Version of the Bible*, edited by Bruce M. Metzger, (New York: Oxford University Press, 1990). New Revised Standard Version Bible, copyright 1989, Division of Christian Education of the National Council of the Churches of Christ in the United States of America. Used by permission. All rights reserved.

and Obed the father of Jesse, [6] and Jesse the father of King David. And David was the father of Solomon by the wife of Uriah, [7] and Solomon the father of Rehoboam, and Rehoboam the father of Abijah, and Abijah the father of Asaph, [8] and Asaph the father of Jehoshaphat, and Jehoshaphat the father of Joram, and Joram the father of Uzziah, [9] and Uzziah the father of Jotham, and Jotham the father of Ahaz, and Ahaz the father of Hezekiah, [10] and Hezekiah the father of Manasseh, and Manasseh the father of Amos, and Amos the father of Josiah, [11] and Josiah the father of Jechoniah and his brothers, at the time of the deportation to Babylon. [12] And after the deportation to Babylon: Jechoniah was the father of Salathiel, and Salathiel the father of Zerubbabel, [13] and Zerubbabel the father of Abiud, and Abiud the father of Eliakim, and Eliakim the father of Azor, [14] and Azor the father of Zadok, and Zadok the father of Achim, and Achim the father of Eliud, [15] and Eliud the father of Eleazar, and Eleazar the father of Matthan, and Matthan the father of Jacob, [16] and Jacob the father of Joseph the husband of Mary, of whom Jesus was born, who is called the Messiah.

Read

Usually when this Gospel is read in church, eyes begin to glaze over. All those strange names! It can be a nightmare for the person who has not read over the text before reading it in public. However, it is very important as it occurs at the very beginning of Matthew's Gospel and is intended to show Jesus as the continuation of the story of God's dealings with Israel and the fulfilment of all the promises God made to this people. This list of names, not to be taken literally as Jesus' antecedents, is a summary of the Old Testament, of which the birth of the long awaited Messiah (the Christ) is the culmination. The list expresses Matthew's conviction that God works through all that is human in order to bring the divine plan of salvation to fulfilment. Human life does have meaning, even though the meaning is not always possible to discern.

Matthew clearly understands Joseph to be the legal adoptive father of Jesus, not his biological father. The abrupt change at the end of the text from "X was the father of Y" to "Joseph the husband of Mary, of whom Jesus was born" (1:16), tells us that this last relationship is very different from all that have gone before. However, Joseph is still very important in Matthew's scheme of things, because it is through the adoption that Jesus can claim to be "son of David", the great king whose reign would continue forever in the person whom later generations would look forward to as the Messiah, which is the meaning of the word "Christ". In the translation used above, the word "Christ" is always translated as "Messiah". Jesus is therefore the royal heir to the throne promised long ago by God.

There are five women mentioned in the list and all of them had some sort of irregular relationships. Their inclusion may seek to point out that God has not always followed human laws but sometimes gone beyond them to further the divine purposes. Four of the five, the exception being Mary, were Gentiles (non-Jews). Therefore we see that Jesus' own family is inclusive of other nations, which presages his mission to the whole world.

The genealogy changes dramatically at the end in order to stress the essential difference between Jesus and all the others who have gone before him. God has acted continually throughout history, but in Christ something unique has happened. We are not told, as in Luke's Gospel, anything about the immediate lead up to this miraculous event of the virgin birth. We have to take Mathew's text as it was written and try to find out what God may be saying to us through it. The Bible is made up of all sorts of different kinds of writing. God has something to say through each bit, but to get the whole picture we have to take everything into account while respecting the particular text in front of us.

Reflect

Read again the text of *Matthew* 1:1-16 slowly.

What does God want to say to me (to us) at this moment by means of this text? What strikes you about this list of names? Are there some names you recognise? What do you think the title "Messiah" means? To help our reflection and the application of the Word of God to daily life, I will propose some more questions. This is not a test. There is neither one particular correct answer nor a wrong one. Your answers might help you to deepen your relationship with God. Take whatever time you need for each question:

1. Think back over your own family tree and pray for your ancestors. Can you discern the presence of God at work in your family?
2. Do you think Joseph was a good father to Jesus?
3. If you are a mother or father, ask God to help you live your vocation as well as possible. Are you a good mother or father?
4. If you have living parents, how do you treat them?

5. If you are married, how do you treat your spouse?
6. If you live in community, how do you treat your brothers and sisters?
7. This list of names tells us nothing about the feelings of Mary and Joseph. What do you think they felt about their particular parts in God's plan of salvation?

Respond

What does your heart want to say to God now? What do you feel? There is no feeling that is unacceptable. Prayer is a relationship with God and every relationship is different. We see in the psalms a great variety of human emotions in relation to God. Perhaps some of the words below respond to what you feel.

Praise, O servants of the Lord,
Praise the name of the Lord!
May the name of the Lord be blessed
Both now and for evermore!
From the rising of the sun to its setting
Praised be the name of the Lord!

High above all nations is the Lord,
Above the heavens his glory.
Who is like the Lord, our God,
Who has risen on high to his throne
Yet stoops from the heights to look down,
To look down upon heaven and earth?

From the dust he lifts up the lowly,
From his misery he raises the poor
To set him in the company of princes,
Yes, with the princes of his people.
To the childless wife he gives a home
And gladdens her heart with children.[4]

It is important to give yourself some space so that your heart has the opportunity to speak directly to God with your own words, even if these do not seem to be as beautiful as those of Sacred Scripture. What does your heart want to say to God?

---

4   Psalm 112 (113) in the *Grail* version.

Rest

Most people would agree that life today tends to be rather hectic. What happened to all those "must haves", all those time-saving machines that would change our lives for the better? We have to admit that washing machines, microwave ovens and so on, do save a lot of time but where does the time go? Perhaps you spend all the time you save on other "time-saving" devices like the computer, or the mobile phone, or the iPod (whatever that is!).

We seem to have less time than ever to do more and more things. I had to do a lot of travelling in recent years visiting Carmelite communities throughout the world. On a plane, despite all the inconveniences, at least no one could get hold of me through the usual time-saving media! In some parts of the world there is a lack of the amenities that many people take for granted. Electricity can be shut-off for hours on end. It is not too much of a problem during the day, but at night when there is no light you might as well go to bed.

When for some reason you are cut off from the usual things that fill your day, what do you do? Can it possibly be that you might allow God to break through your busy schedule? We can become so busy that we can forget about what is truly important. In the Scripture text above that we have been using for prayer we have seen that Jesus, Mary and Joseph are part of a people, a community, a family. Much more important than the things that we possess is who we are. Each one of us is the fruit of a long line of people. Many of the names in the genealogy of Jesus are no more than that; we do not know much about them, whilst others have a story behind them. Through all the ups and downs of history God is working out the divine plan of salvation for creation. We can choose to tune into this plan or work against it. However, God uses even sin to fulfil the divine purpose. It is usually very difficult to understand what God is up to and it becomes more difficult when we are trying to swim against the current. It is much better to try to go with the flow.

Many people nowadays are interested in their family tree. Life is fragile, and if your great- great- great-grandfather had not survived the outbreak of illness that carried off his brothers and sisters, you would not be reading this. Is life just a lottery, or does your life have some meaning? The followers of Jesus Christ believe that only in God can we find meaning. God has created you for a purpose. Perhaps you have found that purpose already, or perhaps you are still searching. Listen to God in the silence of your heart in order to learn that you are loved.

MARY IN THE GENEALOGY OF JESUS

This part of the *Lectio Divina* process is an invitation to let go of our own words and thoughts, no matter how profound they may be. We are also invited to put down the Bible and simply rest in the Word of God, which goes beyond human words.

Act

Prayer is not an isolated practice; it must have some effect in one's life. The fruit of prayer can be discerned in the midst of daily life. Today pray for your family, including those members you have never met, or perhaps even better, those you do not like. Make sure you do something nice for someone close to you.

Prayer is a relationship with God, and so it is important to listen to what God wants to say to us. What is God saying to us in the figure of Mary? We have prayed with a text of Scripture that acts like a bridge from the Old Testament to the New Testament. It tells us that Jesus is part of the Chosen People and is indeed the long-awaited Messiah. There were many ideas about who and what the Messiah would be, but God has done something beyond all human expectations. Jesus is "Son of David" through Joseph's adoption of him. Mary is Jesus' mother but he has no human father.

It is not possible for us to grasp hold of God with our human intellect because God "lives in inaccessible light" (*1 Timothy* 6:16). However, God has revealed something of the divine plan of salvation in the stories and prophecies of the Old Testament. God chooses certain people throughout history to further this plan. Mary is chosen and she responds to God's plan with total openness and availability. Matthew's Gospel tells us nothing about how Mary felt, but it does tell us the result of God's choice of her to be the mother of the Messiah. She consented to her place in God's plan even though what she was asked to do was so unusual and indeed dangerous. Joseph, the man to whom she was legally bound, was not the father of her child, but it was through him that Jesus could be recognised as "son of David", which was one of the traditional titles of the Messiah.

In Mary we find the fulfilment of the double-sided mission of the Chosen People: to bring forth and to welcome the Messiah in faith. The Old Testament is the story of God's love for the Chosen People who were chosen to be a light to the nations of the world. This mission is focused in the person of the Messiah.

Each person in the genealogy plays his or her part, whether consciously or not, in the lead-up to the birth of the Messiah, but above all Mary has a vital and immediate role as the Virgin Mother of Jesus the Christ. Ask her to help you today to live the way her Son has taught.

The betrothal of Mary and Joseph.
Ceramic by Adam Kossowski in the St. Joseph Chapel at Aylesford Priory,
Kent, England.

MARY AT GOD'S SERVICE
Matthew 1:18-25

Opening Prayer

Loving God, I thank you for the birth of your Son as one of us. Thank you for Mary, his mother, and for Joseph who accepted Jesus as his son, following your will, which you revealed to him in a dream. Help me to be open to your will and to hear your voice through your Word.

Text

Read attentively the following Scripture text for the first time in order to get an idea of the overall sense and to take in the details. The text below is taken from the *New Jerusalem Bible*, which is a translation by Catholic scholars dating from 1985.[5] It has become the most widely-used Catholic Bible outside the U.S.A.

> [18] This is how Jesus Christ came to be born. His mother Mary was betrothed to Joseph; but before they came to live together she was found to be with child through the Holy Spirit. [19] Her husband Joseph, being an upright man and wanting to spare her disgrace, decided to divorce her informally. [20] He had made up his mind to do this when suddenly the angel of the Lord appeared to him in a dream and said, 'Joseph son of David, do not be afraid to take Mary home as your wife, because she has conceived what is in her by the Holy Spirit. [21] She will give birth to a son and you must name him Jesus, because he is the one who is to save his people from their sins.' [22] Now all this took place to fulfil what the Lord had spoken through the prophet: [23] Look! the virgin is with child and will give birth to a son whom they will call Immanuel, a name which means 'God-is-with-us'. [24] When Joseph woke up he did what the angel of the Lord had told him to do: he took his wife to his home; [25] he had not had intercourse with her when she gave birth to a son; and he named him Jesus.

---

5   *The New Jerusalem Bible*, edited by Henry Wansbrough, O.S.B., (London: Darton, Longman & Todd, 1985) © Darton, Longman & Todd Ltd. and Doubleday & Company Ltd. a division of Random House, Inc.; used with permission.

Read

We are told in this passage that Mary and Joseph were betrothed. This was a legally binding arrangement and the couple were recognised as husband and wife, though they had not as yet begun to live together. Even at this stage, the bond could only be broken by death or divorce, and unfaithfulness was considered to be adultery. There was normally a period of about a year before the couple lived together. Joseph discovered that Mary was pregnant. According to the Law of Moses, adultery was punishable by death. In the book of *Deuteronomy* (22:23-27), death by stoning is mandated. By Joseph's time, the penalty had been mitigated but it was still severe.

We are told that Joseph was righteous, or just, or as in the present translation "an upright man". In Matthew's Gospel, this means someone who follows God's law. Traditionally there have been three suggestions regarding the state of Joseph's knowledge: the first, that Joseph discovered somehow that Mary was pregnant and believed that she had committed adultery but because of his love and respect for her, he decided to divorce her in an informal way; the second, that Joseph was told of Mary's pregnancy. He believed in Mary's innocence but could not square this with the facts and so he preferred to withdraw from the marriage; the third, that Joseph knew that Mary was pregnant by the work of God's Spirit and decided to withdraw from the marriage lest he interfere with God's will.

There is some debate about the next phrase, "wanting to spare her disgrace". Strictly speaking the word that Matthew uses simply means to 'unveil' or 'reveal', and it does not necessarily have a negative connotation. If the third suggestion about Joseph's understanding of the situation is correct, it would refer to his unwillingness to make this mystery public. There is a problem with the idea of an informal divorce. This seems always to have been a public act before witnesses and so it is difficult to see in what sense the act could have been informal. The text could mean 'secretly separate himself'.

Joseph then, for whatever reason, decides to move out of the picture. However, God has other plans. The angel of the Lord appears to him in a dream and tells him to take Mary to his home as his wife because she has conceived by the power of the Holy Spirit. The angel says, "Do not be afraid". This is a common phrase in both the Old and the New Testaments when a human being is faced by a divine manifestation. Did Joseph experience a 'holy fear' in the presence of the mystery of Mary's virginal pregnancy? Was he already aware that she had conceived by the power of the Holy Spirit and so the dream was to instruct him to have no fear but that he was indeed an important part of God's plan and he was to take Mary as his wife? If that were true, then the angel does not reveal to Joseph that Mary has virginally conceived; instead the angel confirms what Joseph already knows, but tells him that God's plan for him is to be the husband of Mary and the guardian of Jesus, whom he will name. Even though Joseph is not the father, he must perform the primary task of a Jewish father by naming the child. In this way Joseph becomes the legitimate and legal father of Jesus. The focus in this text is on Joseph's role. Because Joseph is a descendant of King David, Jesus does not lack an essential credential of the Messiah of Israel.

Matthew uses a prophecy of the prophet Isaiah (*Isaiah* 7:14) and applies it to Jesus. In its original Old Testament setting it was a prophecy that the country would be delivered from its enemies before the child of a young woman could grow up and reach the age of reason. In the Greek translation of the Old Testament from the original Hebrew, about 200 years before Christ, the word "young woman" is changed to "virgin" and it is this Greek translation that Matthew uses. This child was given the symbolic name, "Immanuel", which means 'God is with us'. Matthew understands Jesus as the fulfilment of the Scriptures, and he feels free to use his Bible to illustrate this. Matthew believes that, in Jesus, God is with us.

Joseph is obedient to the angel's message and names the child. This act makes Jesus a member of 'the house of David', a successor to the great King David. Matthew makes very clear again that Joseph is not the biological father of Jesus, but says nothing about the relationship between Mary and Joseph later. From very early on there was a strong tradition that Mary remained always a virgin.

Matthew is speaking to his own community of convert Jews in this story. God, through an angel, intervenes in the story to ensure the divine plan of salvation. Joseph is given the command to name the child "Jesus", which was the same name as 'Joshua'. Matthew expected his readers to understand that Jesus was like the Old Testament Joshua, the successor of Moses (*Numbers* 27:12-23; *Deuteronomy* 31:7-23; *Joshua* 1:5-9).

Reflect

Read again the text of *Matthew* 1:18-25.

What strikes you about this story? What do you think is the main point Matthew wants to get over? God speaks to each one of us especially through the words of Scripture. These ancient stories are not just stories of people who lived long ago. They are about us, so what might God be saying to our present situation through this story of the holy family? I will suggest some questions that might be helpful in teasing out the meaning of the story for us.

1. Do you consider yourself to be an "upright" person? What does that mean in your daily life?
2. What is more important, the letter of the law or what your conscience is telling you? How does that show itself in practice?
3. Do you judge people whom you consider to have been immoral in some way? Are you sure?
4. Are you open to God's action in your life?
5. Can you trace God's action in your life so far?
6. Does God enter into your relationships?

Respond

Having been through these questions and the text about the circumstances surrounding the birth of Jesus, what is in your heart? Do you want to thank God for your family or complain about them? Are you confused about what God is doing in your life and in the world? Only you know how you feel, and only you can respond to God from your heart. Below I have suggested a prayer that might get you started, or perhaps the picture preceding the reflection might move you to respond to God.

> *Father, all-powerful and ever living God,*
> *We do well always and everywhere to give you thanks.*
>
> *By a wonderful and inexpressible mystery*
> *The Blessed Virgin Mary conceived your only Son*
> *And bore in her pure womb the Lord of heaven.*
>
> *She who knew not man becomes a mother;*
> *She who has given birth remains a virgin.*
> *What joy is hers at your twofold gift:*
> *She is full of wonder at her virgin-motherhood*
> *And full of joy at giving birth to the Redeemer.*
>
> *Through him the angels of heaven*
> *Offer their prayer of adoration*
> *As they rejoice in your presence for ever.*
> *May our voices be one with theirs*

In their triumphant hymn of praise:

Holy, holy, holy Lord, God of power and might,
Heaven and earth are full of your glory.
Hosanna in the highest.
Blessed is he who comes in the name of the Lord.
Hosanna in the highest. [6]

Rest

Just because we go to church or say a few prayers is not a guarantee that everything will go our way. There is the old story of the man who had grave financial difficulties and so decided to pray that he might win the lottery and so solve the crisis in which he found himself. He prayed fervently that God might smile on him and that the first prize might fall into his lap. After a few weeks of no luck, he gave up praying as completely useless. However, it turned out that the man had so much faith in his prayers that he had not even bought a lottery ticket!

We are told that Joseph was "an upright man" and yet he found himself in a very delicate situation. Both he and Mary must have suffered greatly as they pondered what future lay in store for them. Being close to God did not spare them from difficulties. Some people look to God to solve their problems but that is not the way God works. We find ourselves in this world as it is with all it joys and all its sorrows. God does not take us out of this world but gives us the possibility of living here in a meaningful way.

Prayer is the way we communicate with God and there are as many ways of praying as there are ways of communicating. We pray as we can. There are no doubt many reasons for reading this book, but perhaps one reason is that you are interested in *Lectio Divina* as a way of prayer. The different movements of this way are not rigid steps to be accomplished; they are not guarantees to achieve something special. The four or five traditional movements of *Lectio Divina* are intended to finally open us to the gift of intimacy with God that is proved, not in spiritual highs, but in the midst of daily life. [7]

Mary obviously was in communication with God, as we have been told in the text that she was with child through the Holy Spirit. Matthew's Gospel maintains

---

6   *Collection of Masses of the Blessed Virgin Mary*, (New York: Catholic Book Publishing Co., 1992), Vol. I, p. 109.

7   The Christian contemplative tradition speaks of four traditional steps of *Lectio Divina*: lectio, meditatio, oratio and contemplatio. I have translated these as: read, reflect, respond and rest. I have also added another step that is often used: act.

a silence about how this could have come about. We are also told that Joseph is in communication with God through a dream. Often in the Bible we read of God communicating through dreams. Many psychologists believe that dreams are highly significant and can tell us a lot about our inner life. However, God also uses other ways to communicate with us, but we need to be on the same wavelength in order to receive these communications. Words are only a small part of human communication, and in order to really grasp what someone else is trying to get across we have to listen to what they are saying without words.

God listens to our words of course but above all reads our hearts. In the Bible the heart is the innermost part of the human being. The *Book of Proverbs* tells us: "Above all else guard your heart for it is the wellspring of life" (4:23). Jesus tells us, "Blessed are the pure in heart for they will see God" (Matthew 5:8). Sometimes we can use words as a barrier against people and against God. If we talk enough, we will not have to listen to what the other person (or God) wants to say to us. In all human communication silence is a valuable tool so that we can really listen to what the other is saying. Silence is also an important part of prayer.

Sometimes difficult situations bring us to silence because words seem so inadequate. Try now to be silent before God, opening your heart to the divine presence.

Act

There are five players in the biblical scene we have been considering: Joseph, Mary, Jesus, the angel and the Holy Spirit. God's Spirit has brought about this miraculous event, which is revealed to Joseph by the angel. Jesus is the Immanuel, 'God with us'. Mary is silent but she consents to God's will and so opens the way for our salvation. How can you consent to God's will in your own life today?

Salvation is the work of God but is made concrete in the co-operation of human beings. How can you co-operate with God today?

The three magi worship the child Jesus.
Woodcut from the printing (c.1484) by Heinrich Knoblochtzer
of The Three Kings of Cologne *by John of Hildesheim, O.Carm.*

THE CHILD AND HIS MOTHER
Matthew 2:11-21

Opening Prayer

Gracious and Loving God, you call all people to live in harmony with one another and with you. Pour your balm of peace into our world of violence so that children may be allowed to grow up securely and surrounded by love. Let your Word touch the hearts of all so that we may do your will in this world.

Text

Read attentively the following Bible text for the first time in order to get an idea of the overall sense and to take in the details.

The text in this reflection comes from the *New King James Version* of the Bible.[8] This is an update of an ancient version compiled in England in 1611. The king referred to is James VI of Scotland (1567-1625) who took over the English throne as well in 1603, and in England is known as James I. This was the most influential Bible translation in the English language for hundreds of years. It was also possibly the most widely read and best-known book ever published in English. Obviously, as the English language developed the *King James Version* began to become rather old-fashioned, and the need was felt to put it into more modern English while trying to preserve something of its original beauty. Therefore in 1975 a new version was commissioned. Many experts worked on it and finally it was published in 1982.

[11] And when they had come into the house, they (the Magi) saw the young Child with Mary His mother, and fell down and worshiped Him. And when they had opened their treasures, they presented gifts to Him: gold, frankincense, and myrrh. [12] Then, being divinely warned in a dream that they should not return to Herod, they departed for their own country another way. [13] Now when they had departed, behold, an angel of the Lord appeared to Joseph in a dream, saying, "Arise, take the young Child and His mother, flee to

---

Egypt, and stay there until I bring you word; for Herod will seek the young Child to destroy Him." [14] When he arose, he took the young Child and His mother by night and departed for Egypt, [15] and was there until the death of Herod, that it might be fulfilled which was spoken by the Lord through the prophet, saying, "Out of Egypt I called My Son." [16] Then Herod, when he saw that he was deceived by the wise men, was exceedingly angry; and he sent forth and put to death all the male children who were in Bethlehem and in all its districts, from two years old and under, according to the time which he had determined from the wise men. [17] Then was fulfilled what was spoken by Jeremiah the prophet, saying: [18] "A voice was heard in Ramah, Lamentation, weeping, and great mourning, Rachel weeping for her children, Refusing to be comforted, Because they are no more." [19] But when Herod was dead, behold, an angel of the Lord appeared in a dream to Joseph in Egypt, [20] saying, "Arise, take the young Child and His mother, and go to the land of Israel, for those who sought the young Child's life are dead." [21] Then he arose, took the young Child and His mother, and came into the land of Israel.

Read

This is the story of the visit of the Magi (or wise men) to Jesus. They make the mistake of going to King Herod to ask for directions. They assume wrongly that he will be just as excited as they are about the new born king. However, they were wrong. History tells us that Herod was a bloodthirsty despot who would brook no rival for his throne. He even killed his own children because he perceived them to be a threat. There is no independent evidence outside of the Gospel for the slaughter of the innocents but the action seems to fit in with what we know of Herod's character. However, the main point that Matthew is making by means of this story is that God was active in the life of Jesus from the very beginning. The Gospels are a different way of writing than that in the daily newspapers. The Gospels seek to lead people to faith in Christ, or confirm their faith, and they do this in a variety of ways, one of which is the story form.

Herod represents the resistance of this world to the divine kingship of Jesus. The story of the life of Jesus being in danger from birth, and the sojourn in Egypt, is Matthew's way of underlining another parallel between Jesus and Moses. The experience of the holy family in this story would have spoken very powerfully to many members of Matthew's community who had suffered persecution and exile for the sake of Jesus.

It is important not to try to harmonise this story with what we know from the Gospel of Luke. Each presents different traditions for different reasons in order to say something distinct about Jesus. Let us focus for the moment on what God may be saying to us through the Gospel of Matthew.

This story speaks of the sad reality that his own people in general rejected Jesus, while it was the pagans who welcomed him. The multitude of people who make up the Church are represented by the wise men.

One of the striking things about this passage, at least from our perspective of looking at texts in which Mary features, is that she is never named. However, she is mentioned five times always in the same formula: "the young Child and his mother" (2:11, 13, 14, 20, 21). Matthew is careful not to say that Joseph is the father of Jesus. Jesus and Mary appear always together and never apart.

Reflect

Read again the text of *Matthew* 2:11-21.

What are the main elements of this well-known story? What is particularly striking for you? What might God be saying to you by means of this piece of Scripture? This is a level that goes beyond the information that we can glean from the passage. We are seeking a word of life. To help in this process, I suggest some questions below. There are no right or wrong answers. There are simply your answers, which are between you and God. Perhaps God will show you something about yourself in your answers. This might be important, so please do not reject too quickly what seems to be coming through in your answers to the questions.

1. The wise men recognised the One they had been searching for in the young child. Think of a young child (your own or a child of your friends). What could God possibly be saying to you through him or her?
2. The wise men presented gifts. Do you give gifts? Why? To give pleasure, or to buy affection or ensure support?
3. God communicated to the wise men and to Joseph through a dream. How does God communicate with you? Are your various channels of communication open?
4. The innocents continue to be slaughtered. How do you protect life?

5. Mary cared for her young child. Do you care for someone? How does this actually affect your life?

6. The holy family were refugees. What do you think of refugees in your country? Do you think refugees feel welcome in your country? If not, what can you do about it?

Respond

This is the moment to lay aside all that is going through your head and allow your heart to respond to God. Only you know what your heart wants to say. The prayer below might get you started. Leave it aside too if and when you no longer need it.

> *May you be blessed, my daughter, by God Most High, beyond all women on earth. The trust which you have shown will not pass from human hearts, as they commemorate the power of God for evermore. God grant you may be always held in honour and rewarded with blessings, since you did not consider your own life when our nation was brought to its knees, but warded off our ruin, walking in the right path before our God.*[9]

Rest

In western countries there is an impending crisis caused by the very low birth rate. We will shortly become top-heavy with retired people. This will bring many social problems in its wake. At the same time a huge number of abortions are carried out. Children and the very old are the most vulnerable to violence and abuse of every sort. The slaughter of the innocents is not restricted to biblical times but is an ever present reality in our 'civilised' societies.

The mystery of evil stalks our world. When we are really honest we can glimpse the possibility for every evil in the depths of our own heart. That can be shocking, but is in fact liberating. We no longer self-righteously condemn other people but we can understand that their actions are the result of a chain of events, some of which were out of their control. We begin to love the sinner while still hating the sin, because we realise that 'there but for the grace of God go I'. While continuing to struggle against evil in all its forms, we leave all judgement to God. Condemnation of others is destructive of our own peace. When we go to prayer we can take all these concerns and issues and place them

---

9   *Judith* 13:18-20 (text from the *New Jerusalem Bible*).

in God's hands for we are certainly not going to solve them. Our best approach is silence, for in silence we become gradually conformed to the mind of Christ.

Silence, however, is not easy to attain, and when we eventually achieve some silence it is not at all easy to maintain. First of all, what is so good about silence? Why should we want to be silent? In *Psalm* 62 we are invited to wait in silence for God. We are surrounded by so much noise that it is difficult for us to discern God's voice. Therefore the first reason to seek some silence in our lives is that it helps us swim through the deluge of words in daily life and helps us follow where God is drawing us. Many words and noise of various descriptions can be used as a barrier against what we do not want to hear. When we pray, we are entering into a relationship with God. We hope that God listens to us and we should reciprocate by listening to what God wants to say to us. Of course, God speaks through the Bible and the sacraments, but God also speaks in many other ways – through the people we meet and the situations in which we find ourselves, as well as in the problems of our world, big and small.

In Matthew's Gospel Mary is silent and so is able to discern the will of God despite the fact that it is so extraordinary. We often impose upon God our own will in very subtle ways: 'This is what I want and so it must be what God wants!' We can protect ourselves from the will of God by not listening and so not allowing God's Word to pierce our armour. Take a few moments now to rest in the Word of God. You do not have to think about anything in particular; you do not have to do anything. Simply be there before God and open your heart to the divine purpose.

Act

Make a choice for life today. Try to put into practice what you believe God is asking of you.

Mary in the Gospel of Mark

The Evangelist Mark depicted as a winged lion.
Ceramic by Adam Kossowski in St. Joseph's Chapel, Aylesford Priory, Kent, England.

Mark limits his Gospel to the public activity of Jesus and does not speak of his origins. It is generally accepted by scholars that Mark's is the first Gospel to be written, and that both Matthew and Luke use it to some extent as well as other sources. There is a very early tradition that Mark depended on the recollections of Saint Peter and that he wrote in Rome. It seems that Mark wrote his Gospel sometime between 60 and 70 A.D. and that his intended hearers or readers were predominantly Gentile (non-Jewish) Christians.

Mark was not writing biography; instead he was interested in proclaiming that Jesus was the Son of God, and he had to explain why he was crucified. He describes the way of Jesus as the way of suffering, and all who would follow him must be prepared to take up their cross and follow him. The very first proclamation of the Gospel focused exclusively on the Good News about Jesus Christ, and so there are only a few indirect allusions to his Mother.

In the whole of Mark's Gospel we find the name of "Mary" only once (6:3) and it is used for the mother of Jesus. She is also mentioned in the text immediately below, but is simply called "his mother" (3:31). It seems that Mark is only interested in the conflict that existed between Jesus and his natural family. Jesus establishes a new family based on faith.

In several places the Synoptic Gospels (*Matthew, Mark* and *Luke*) have the same story. Sometimes it is changed from one to the other, and it can be interesting to note these differences as they can tell us something about the particular evangelist's point of view.

A thirteenth-century icon of 'Mary, Mother and Lady of Carmel', from one of the Order's ancient churches in Cyprus, now in the Museo Macarios I in Nicosia. In the painting Our Lady wraps her mantle around the Carmelite friars (bottom left) who look to her for protection.

JESUS AND HIS FAMILY

Mark 3:31-35; Luke 8:19-21; Matthew 12:46-50

Opening Prayer

Eternal God, you have called us into your family, made up of all those who hear your word and live it. Help us to be open to Jesus, your Son, and his message, that we may have life in abundance.

Text

In this reflection there are three Scripture texts from three different Gospels, all telling the same story from a different angle. Read attentively the following texts for the first time in order to get an idea of the overall sense and to take in the details. The first text, from Mark's Gospel, is taken from the *English Standard Version*. This is intended to be a rather literal translation of the Bible with a modern expression. The text of Saint Luke's Gospel is taken from the Bible in 'basic English', which tries to get over the biblical message using the simplest words possible so that it could be useful in countries where English is used but is not the first language. The third text, from Matthew's Gospel, is taken from an old translation by John Nelson Darby; he attempted to provide a simple but exact translation in English from the original biblical languages.

Mark 3 (English Standard Version) [10]

[31] And his mother and his brothers came, and standing outside they sent to him and called him. [32] And a crowd was sitting around him, and they said to him, "Your mother and your brothers are outside, seeking you." [33] And he answered them, "Who are my mother and my brothers?" [34] And looking about at those who sat around him, he said, "Here are my mother and my brothers! [35] Whoever does the will of God, he is my brother and sister and mother."

Luke 8 (Bible in Basic English) [11]

---

10 *ESV Bible, (The Holy Bible, English Standard Version)* © 2001 Crossway Bibles, a publishing ministry of Good News Publishers. Used by permission; all rights reserved.
11 *The Basic Bible, Containing the Old and New Testaments in Basic English*, edited by S. H. Hooke, (Cambridge: Cambridge University Press, 1949 & 1965). Reprinted with permission.

[19] And his mother and his brothers came to him, and they were not able to get near him because of the great number of people. [20] And someone said to him, Your mother and your brothers are outside desiring to see you. [21] But he said to them in answer, My mother and my brothers are those who have knowledge of the word of God and do it.

Matthew 12 (The Darby Bible)[12]

[46] But while he was yet speaking to the crowds, behold, his mother and his brethren stood without, seeking to speak to him. [47] Then one said unto him, Behold, thy mother and thy brethren are standing without, seeking to speak to thee. [48] But he answering said to him that spoke to him, Who is my mother, and who are my brethren? [49] And, stretching out his hand to his disciples, he said, Behold my mother and my brethren; [50] for whosoever shall do the will of my Father who is in the heavens, he is my brother, and sister, and mother.

Read

This is the story of the visit of Jesus' family to him. Mark does show that there was some sort of conflict between Jesus and his family. Like the other evangelists, Mark is not concerned about writing biographies and he does not have the same questions that we have in our minds. Therefore he does not necessarily tell us what we want to hear but what we need to hear. The other evangelists do refer to differences in the family but they do have another slant on the story (*Matthew* 12:46-50; *Luke* 2:35, 48-50; *John* 2:4). In Matthew's case it is exactly the same story as appears in Mark, but the former seems to soften it somewhat.

Mark tells us a little earlier (3:21) that the family of Jesus went to get him and take him by force because people were saying that he was mad. Mark was writing for a community that had to suffer these very same things. When they were converted to faith in Jesus Christ, no doubt many had to face the suspicion that they had gone mad. Perhaps some of their families tried to take them away by force. Mark is telling his community, in the words of Jesus, that their true family is made up of fellow believers.

---

12 *The Holy Scriptures: A New Translation from the Original Languages* by J. N. Darby (1890).

There is no mention of Jesus' father in this story. The simplest reason would be that Joseph had died some time previously, but at the beginning of the Gospel Mark has called Jesus "Son of God" (1:1) so perhaps there is a hint here of that truth. Who are these brothers of Jesus? There is no mention of sisters. Again the simplest answer would be that they are blood brothers, either children of Joseph by a previous marriage, or even children of Mary and Joseph. It is true that in Jesus' time the word "brothers" had a number of meanings. From the text itself we cannot be sure what relationship these "brothers" had with Jesus, but we have to keep in mind that this Gospel, like the others, was written from within a community and received by the Church as a whole. A very early and strong tradition states that Mary remained a virgin and therefore her only child was Jesus.

In Mark, the scene contributes to the sense of rising opposition against Jesus. Scribes come down from Jerusalem and declare that Jesus is controlled by the prince of devils. His family comes to him "to restrain him" (3:31; cf. 3:21), and while the crowd is around Jesus, his family is outside. Jesus responds, first asking who his mother and brothers are, and then announcing the formation of a new family: "Whoever does the will of God is my brother and sister and mother" (3:35).

Luke places this same scene in a positive context. It comes after the parable of the sower and the different kinds of soil. There is a complete set of examples of those who hear the Word of God and do it: the Twelve; the group of women who followed Jesus; the disciples; and finally the family of Jesus.

Luke omits the reference to the efforts of Jesus' family to restrain him (*Mark* 3:20-21). Luke also compresses the scene, omitting any reference to Jesus' sisters, the contrast between the family outside and the crowd seated around Jesus. The result is that Jesus' apparent rejection of his physical family has been cut out from the Gospel story, while leaving his statement in place that those who hear and do the Word of God are in fact members of his family. This positive portrayal of Jesus' family goes well with the role of Mary in the infancy narrative, and in *Luke* 11:27-28, and *Acts* 1:14. Luke says nothing about the family's motive in coming to Jesus, and explains their position outside as being due to the impossibility of getting near him due to the crowd.

Matthew is not interested in biographical details, and his whole thrust is to present the Good News about Jesus the Messiah. He takes up the stories and sayings that he has received and he uses these to show that Jesus is the Son of God who has come to proclaim the presence of the Kingdom of God. In order to enter this Kingdom one must do the will of the Father, towards whom Jesus' whole life is directed. Jesus' disciples become members of his family inasmuch as they do the will of the Father. In this way they become like the Son.

The Jews are the chosen people and claimed physical descent from Abraham. Jesus was rejected by his own people and he declares that his family are all those who hear the Word of God and put it into practice.

Reflect

Read again *Mark* 3:31-35; *Luke* 8:19-21; and *Matthew* 12:46 -50.

What strikes you about the story that is told in three slightly different ways? Can you identify any common elements? What do you think is the principal point behind the story? The questions below are intended to help you translate these Scripture passages into the reality of your daily life. Do not feel you have to answer them all. Perhaps one question will grab your attention. If so, stay with it for a while.

1. How does the Word of God come to you in your daily life?
2. What does it mean for you to do the will of God?
3. How do you balance your faith and your obligations to your family?
4. Believers in Christ are his brothers and sisters. What can you do to treat other Christians as your brothers and sisters?

Respond

Perhaps you are moved to pray for your family or others who are dear to you. Let your heart respond to God's Word in whatever way you feel drawn. Praying with beads is a venerable custom in many religions.[13] You might like to try it. The unrushed, rhythmic repeating of the *Our Father* and the ten *Hail Marys*, either aloud or in the quiet of one's heart, often leads to silence. What is important is that you communicate with God in whatever way you can.

> *Hail Mary, full of grace,*
> *the Lord is with thee.*
> *Blessed art thou among women*
> *and blessed is the fruit of thy womb, Jesus.*
> *Holy Mary, Mother of God,*

---

13 See the brief but illuminating chapter by Sarah Boss on 'Telling the Beads: The Practice and Symbolism of the Rosary', in Sarah Jane Boss, (ed.), *Mary: The Complete Resource*, (London & New York: Continuum, 2007), pp. 385-94.

pray for us, sinners,
now and at the hour of our death.
Amen.

Rest

The mission of Jesus went beyond his own family and his own people to the whole world. He was sent as the Messiah to Israel, but anyone – from whatever race – who listens to God's Word and acts on it, is counted as a member of Jesus' family.

Listening is not easy. We have our own issues and naturally these are in the forefront of our minds. They can also make it very difficult to really hear what someone else is trying to say to us. Apparently a lot of accidents are caused by people who use their mobile phones while driving. Their attention is not fully focused on what the traffic conditions are telling them because they are intent on their telephone conversation. Sometimes when another person is speaking to us, there is a different conversation going on in our heads. There is a time for speaking, and a time for silence, but as soon as we try to have a bit of silence our heads are full of all sorts of distractions. Some of these can be trivial, but other distractions can point to something important. In our normal daily life we can be so busy that we do not pay attention to important issues. When we quieten down, these issues have a chance to emerge and clamour for our attention. We do need to give some time to whatever might be bothering us. Perhaps we need to look at an important relationship in our lives, or how we really feel about something that has happened to us. However, we do also need time simply to be in silence, because all our concerns, valid and important though they are, can also drown out the still small voice of God.

Members of the same family share a common bond. We are members of the family of God because God is the source of all being. We live and breathe each moment as a gift from God. The tragedy of human existence is that we convince ourselves we are separate from God. This is taken to extremes by those who not only deny their need of God but even deny that God is. An unhealthy secularism tries to force religion to the margins of human society and to banish God from human life. God does not need defenders but witnesses. Believers must bear witness to God by the way they live. Saint Francis of Assisi is reputed to have said that we must preach constantly, and sometimes we must use words. People are subjected to so many empty words and empty promises through the mass media. The example of a committed life will convince many.

We cannot bear witness to God if we allow the daily pressures of life to convince us that God is 'out there' somewhere and that we are left alone to struggle along as best we can. The truth is that we are part of the stream of life that includes all people, and indeed the whole of creation, seen and unseen. This stream of life issues forth from God continually. Therefore, to find God we do not need to shout; we can listen to God in creation, and we can turn inwards to find God.

What do we say to God? No doubt we have all sorts of concerns, but there comes a time when words fail even the most inveterate talker. However, Saint John of the Cross, the Spanish Carmelite poet and mystic, wrote that the language God best hears is silent love.[14]

Try a few minutes of silence. Ask Mary, the Virgin Mother of the Lord, to help you listen to God in the silence. Let go of your own words and thoughts and just be there for God.

Act

We may not have our family forever. Show your appreciation of someone close to you today. As you go about your business, try to hear God's voice in the everyday and put God's will into practice in the small events of your life.

---

14 *Maxims* 53. There are two major translations into English of the complete works of Saint John of the Cross. The older is edited by E. Allison Peers, *The Complete Works of St. John of the Cross*, (London: Burns & Oates, 1954). The more recent is edited by Kieran Kavanaugh, O.C.D., and Otilio Rodriguez, O.C.D., *The Collected Works of St. John of the Cross*, (Washington, D.C.: I.C.S. Publications, 1991).

*An ancient carving of Our Lady of Mount Carmel
at the lower Carmelite Church in Salamanca, Spain.*

REFLECTION 5

JESUS VISITS NAZARETH
Mark 6:1-6a

Opening Prayer

Loving God, in your providence, Nazareth was the home town of your Son Jesus. Send your blessing on all those from my home. Let me open my heart to you in faith so that you might accomplish your will in me. Amen.

Text

Read attentively the following Scripture text for the first time in order to get an idea of the overall sense and to take in the details. The text is from the *New American Bible*, a translation made specifically for the American market.[15] It is a work of Catholic biblical scholars specifically intended for use in public worship, and first published in 1970. There have been second (1986) and third (1991) editions in which the language has been changed somewhat to make it more inclusive. In the year 2000, the New Testament and Psalms were modified again for use in the liturgy.

> [1] He departed from there and came to his native place, accompanied by his disciples. [2] When the sabbath came he began to teach in the synagogue, and many who heard him were astonished. They said, "Where did this man get all this? What kind of wisdom has been given him? What mighty deeds are wrought by his hands! [3] Is he not the carpenter, the son of Mary, and the brother of James and Joses and Judas and Simon? And are not his sisters here with us?" And they took offense at him. [4] Jesus said to them, "A prophet is not without honor except in his native place and among his own kin and in his own house." [5] So he was not able to perform any mighty deed there, apart from curing a few sick people by laying his hands on them. [6] He was amazed at their lack of faith.

15 *The New American Bible*, edited by Louis Hartman and Myles Bourke, available in various editions. The passage is taken from the *New American Bible with Revised New Testament and Revised Psalms* © 1991, 1986, 1970 Confraternity of Christian Doctrine, Washington, D.C. and used by permission of the copyright owner. All Rights Reserved.

Read

This is the story of Jesus' visit to his home village. The population would have been around 1,500-2,000 people, and Jesus had been a craftsman; not impoverished, but also not one of the educated class who could devote himself to study. In the previous chapter of Mark's Gospel we can read of various miracles performed by Jesus, and the response of faith on the part of pagans. Now he comes to his own village, to his own people, amongst whom he has grown up. What will be their reaction? We are told that they were at first astonished at what they saw and heard but their prior knowledge of him got in the way. They took offence at him. Jesus appeared to be an ordinary working man; only someone looking at him with the eyes of faith could get beyond the external appearances.

This scene is a transition from the early success that Jesus' mission seemed to have to the opposition and incredulity that he faced as he continued. Was Mark here reminding his own community that from very early on it was Gentiles who came to faith in Jesus while his own people rejected him, and therefore not to be surprised when they too were rejected? Clearly most, if not all, of Jesus' family lived in Nazareth. Four brothers are mentioned as well as some indeterminate number of sisters. He is known as "the son of Mary" in this account and not the "son of Joseph". This could be because Joseph has been dead a long time, or because the people want to cast some aspersions on his parentage, or perhaps there is another hint that Jesus is more than meets the eye. The "brothers" and "sisters" have some family connection with Jesus but need not be what we understand by the term.

In Jesus' day, when the father died, the eldest son was expected to take over as head of the family. Therefore the actions of Jesus could well have scandalised the village community, and this could have got in the way of faith in him. We know from other sources that the family of Jesus eventually became believers – indeed James became the leader of the Church in Jerusalem – and presumably this was well known to Mark's community.

It is interesting to note that the Gospels of Luke and Matthew have the same scene with variations. Luke (4:16-30) has "Is not this Joseph's son?" (verse 22). In Matthew's version of the scene (13:54-58), he uses the term, "Is not this the carpenter's son? Is not his mother called Mary?" (verse 55). Why did Mark not mention Joseph? Was it simply because Joseph had been dead for some time, or did Mark want to allude to Jesus' real father?

Reflect

Read again the text of *Mark* 6:1-6a.

What are the main elements of this story? What do you find particularly striking? What do you think Jesus expected to find in his home town? The questions below are intended to help you to open your daily life to the Word of God. If you find one useful, stay with it.

1. How did the Word of God first come to you in your home situation?
2. How do you express your faith in wherever you call home now?
3. The local people could not accept Jesus because they thought they knew all about him. How might God be surprising you in your present situation?

Respond

Perhaps the words of Pope Benedict XVI might help you to start your own heart to heart dialogue with God:

> *When Jesus began his public ministry, you had to step aside, so that a new family could grow, the family which it was his mission to establish and which would be made up of those who heard his word and kept it.*[16]

Rest

"The co-efficient of me knowing you reduces my appreciation of what you said by 50%". I have often remembered this saying of a Carmelite that was passed on in the folklore of my religious family. Another, but perhaps harsher way of putting it is: "Familiarity breeds contempt". In other words, "Because I know you, I cannot take you seriously". That is what Jesus suffered when he went home to Nazareth. The townsfolk could not believe that the wee boy they had seen growing up in their midst was the long-awaited Messiah, and so they largely rejected him.

Do you know God? Are you so familiar with some image of God that has been presented to you from school days that you prefer to keep your distance? Can you possibly accept that perhaps the image you have of God is not actually a completely faithful portrait of who God is? Can you let God reshape your whole spiritual life?

---

16   Pope Benedict XVI's encyclical *Spe Salvi (On Christian Hope)* was published in 2007, and is available in various editions.

Prayer is fundamentally a relationship with God.[17] What kind of relationship do you have with God? Is it distant or intimate? Conversation with a person with whom you are rather distant does not tend to flow easily, whereas there is often no need for words when relating to someone who is very close. There are some emotions that cannot easily be put into words. Silence can be awkward if it is the sign that there is nothing to say, but it can also be the way to communicate your deepest feelings in a loving relationship.

We cannot jump into an intimate friendship before we have got to know the other person. God has revealed much in his Word. The Bible tells the story of God's relationship with humanity. We are told that "God loved the world so much that He gave His only Son that whoever believes in him should not be lost but have eternal life" (*John* 3:16). Jesus Christ reveals God in a new way. He has come to make men and women sharers in the divine life. So we have to get to know God, and we do this principally through the revelation that has been given and mediated by the continuing presence of Christ in the Church.

The Christian contemplative tradition is long and immensely rich. It has a vast treasury of how to grow in intimacy with God. There are very many who have gone before us and who have left behind testimony about the journey to God, which is a journey inwards to find God at the very centre of the human soul. When we have found God within, we are sent outwards to serve God in other people. This journey inwards can start at any point when our hearts are sufficiently open to hear the mysterious call of the Beloved.

I invite you to spend a little while listening to the still small voice of God within you. Let go of your own agenda and let God lead you.

Act

Jesus was amazed at the lack of faith displayed by his neighbours. They stopped at the externals and failed to see the possibilities beyond. To take your prayer into your daily life, look for the presence of God in the ordinary things that surround you and in the ordinary events that happen.

---

17   For a brief development of this idea, see Elizabeth Smith & Joseph Chalmers, *A Deeper Love* (London & New York: Continuum, 1999), pp. 11-17.

The Evangelist Luke depicted as a winged bull.
Ceramic by Adam Kossowski in St. Joseph's Chapel, Aylesford Priory, Kent, England.

SECTION THREE:

Mary in the Gospel of Luke

The Gospel according to Luke is part one of a two-part work. The second part is the *Acts of the Apostles*. Tradition tells us that Luke was a companion of Saint Paul on some of his missionary journeys. The large majority of the people for whom he wrote were Gentiles (not Jews). Luke seems to have used Mark's Gospel extensively, but he uses the material in quite a different way, according to his own notable abilities as a story teller. He also used some material that may have been available to Matthew too, as well as some independent sources. A date in the mid-80s A.D. seems likely for the writing of the Gospel.

Luke was probably a Gentile but was very knowledgeable about the Bible. He was writing for Christians of the second generation living outside of Palestine, in contact with a culture and religion different from those within which Jesus operated.

Each Gospel writer has his own particular approach to Jesus, and we must try to hold all of these together and not try to make them all say exactly the same thing. Each Gospel has particular insights that we must not lose. Luke presents Jesus as the compassionate saviour sent to seek and save the lost. The religious leaders reject Jesus, but a small group of disciples are commissioned by the Risen Lord to proclaim the Gospel, and how they do this is detailed in the *Acts of the Apostles*. A great part of the Gospel of Luke is taken up with Jesus' journey to Jerusalem to be crucified, and where he would rise again from the dead. Then, from Jerusalem, the disciples moved out to the ends of the earth and even to the centre of the great empire – Rome itself. The second part of the journey motif is to be found in the *Acts of the Apostles*.

The infancy narratives have no parallel in the other Gospels. While Matthew emphasises the role of Joseph, Luke chooses to stress that of Mary. The genealogy is quite different from that of Matthew, except that they both claim to be that of Joseph. Luke tells us that Jesus was the son, as was supposed, of Joseph (3:23). Luke's portrayal of Mary is a striking example of an important element in the Gospel, that God reverses the poverty and powerlessness of the human condition. Throughout the Gospel of Luke, Mary is portrayed in a positive light as obedient to the Lord (1:39-56; 2:24, 51). Luke uses Our Lady's name "Mary" 12 times, always in the infancy narratives (1:27, 30, 34, 38, 39, 41, 46, 56; 2:5, 16, 19, 34). She is also referred to 7 times as "the mother of Jesus" (1:43; 2:33, 34, 48, 51; 8:19, 20).

*The Annunciation, sculpted by Simon Robinson in 2005,
at Whitefriar Street Carmelite Centre, Dublin.*

THE VOCATION OF MARY

Luke 1:26-38

Opening Prayer

> *O God, you prepared and called Mary to be the Mother of your Son, and she accepted your will with joy. You have a plan for me. Help me to listen to your Word and welcome it into my life. Amen.*

Text

Read attentively the following Bible text for the first time in order to get an idea of the overall sense and to take in the details. The version used for this passage is the *New International Version* (*NIV*), a translation made by more than 100 scholars in contemporary English.[18] It was reviewed and revised by several groups. The goals for the translation were that it be accurate, beautiful, clear and dignified, and that it be suitable both for public and private reading.

26 In the sixth month, God sent the angel Gabriel to Nazareth, a town in Galilee, 27 to a virgin pledged to be married to a man named Joseph, a descendant of David. The virgin's name was Mary. 28 The angel went to her and said, "Greetings, you who are highly favoured! The Lord is with you." 29 Mary was greatly troubled at his words and wondered what kind of greeting this might be. 30 But the angel said to her, "Do not be afraid, Mary, you have found favour with God. 31 You will be with child and give birth to a son, and you are to give him the name Jesus. 32 He will be great and will be called the Son of the Most High. The Lord God will give him the throne of his father David, 33 and he will reign over the house of Jacob for ever; his kingdom will never end." 34 "How will this be," Mary asked the angel, "since I am a virgin?" 35 The angel answered, "The Holy Spirit will come upon you, and the power of the Most High will overshadow you. So the holy one to be born will be called the Son of God. 36 Even Elizabeth your relative is going to have a child in her old age, and she who was said to be barren is in her sixth

---

18 *The Holy Bible, New International Version*, copyright © International Bible Society, 1973, 1978, 1984, used by permission; all rights reserved.

month. [37] For nothing is impossible with God." [38] "I am the Lord's servant," Mary answered. "May it be to me as you have said." Then the angel left her.

Read

This is the famous scene of 'the Annunciation'. It has inspired some of the world's greatest artists. The infancy narrative as a whole is a Gospel in miniature, and a statement of themes that will be developed as the later mission of Jesus unfolds. Luke writes of two annunciations and two births – of John the Baptist and of Jesus. They are compared and contrasted. Can you spot some of the differences between the annunciation to Zechariah of the birth of John the Baptist (*Luke* 1:5-25) and the annunciation to Mary of the birth of Jesus? The annunciations draw upon the pattern of similar events in the Old Testament: the births of Ishmael (*Genesis* 16:7-13), Isaac (*Genesis* 7:1-3, 15-21; 18:1-2, 10-15), and Samson (*Judges* 13:2-23). It is clear that while John will be great, Jesus will be immeasurably greater.

At the Annunciation, God's promises to King David were fulfilled in an unimaginable way. The kingdom that Jesus would establish was not political but a spiritual reality that would last forever. Jesus is not to have a human father but instead he will be Son of God.

As well as being the story of the annunciation of a wonderful birth, it is also the story of Mary's vocation. She is invited to play a part in God's plan of salvation. The first word of the angel to Mary, which in the translation used here is rendered as "Greetings", can mean simply "hello" or it could also mean "rejoice". It seems very likely that Luke wants to impart the idea of an invitation to joy. In the Greek translation of the Old Testament, the same word is used to invite the people to rejoice in the salvation that is coming from God (cf. *Zephaniah* 3:14-15). The joy that was announced by the prophets to Israel at the coming of the Messiah is focused on one particular woman, Mary, who unites in herself the hopes of the people.

The next words of the angel, given in the *New International Version* of the Bible as "you who are highly favoured", have been debated among scholars for many years. It certainly seems that the essential point is that Mary has been transformed by the free action of God (the grace of God) in order to prepare her for her unique mission. The second part of what the angel says, "The Lord is with you", is quite common in the Old Testament. However, it is only used when a command is being issued that is difficult to accomplish, or impossible for a human being (e.g. *Exodus* 3:12). The words extend the promise of God's help in particularly difficult missions. In our text it is aimed at a woman who will give birth. This is always miraculous, but is something that women around the world do every day. The specific assistance of God in the case of Mary is because she will give birth without the intervention of a man. In this case perhaps we can appreciate why Mary was "greatly troubled".

The angel tells Mary not to be afraid because she is specially favoured by God, and the child to whom she will give birth will be great, the Son of the Most High God. He will be the fulfilment of all the promises made by God in the Old Testament. Mary then asks a question about how this is going to happen given the fact that she is a virgin. Like most things in the Bible, there are arguments over the meaning. Some people think that the question is simply a way to move the story on, so that the angel can introduce the miraculous announcement of a virgin birth. Other experts think there is much more to Mary's question, and suggest that it refers to a hidden desire she had to remain a virgin, despite the fact she was legally married to Joseph (though they had not as yet come to live together and share their life). What the angel says next gives a solution to her desire, despite the expectations of her society, for she will be a mother while remaining a virgin.

The "overshadowing" of Mary by God could be an allusion to the cloud (a symbol of God) which covered the tent of the Covenant (*Exodus* 40:35). The angel tells Mary that nothing is impossible for God. This covers the fact of the pregnancy of Elizabeth, for whom it seemed impossible to have a child, as well as the fact that Mary will remain a virgin while becoming a mother.

The acceptance of Mary is a joyous desire that God's will be accomplished in her. She wishes to collaborate totally with God. The joy at the end of this scene corresponds to the invitation to joy at the beginning.

Reflect

Read again the text of *Luke* 1:26-38.

Go through the story again and notice all the details – when, where, who? The angel Gabriel has already appeared in the Gospel of Luke. Where and what did he say, and to whom? What do you think the angel Gabriel means by his words to Mary: "you who are highly favoured" and "The Lord is with you"? Why do you think Mary was troubled? What do you think it means to say that Mary has found favour with God? If it is true that Mary somehow had the desire or felt called to live as a virgin, yet was going through with a normal marriage to Joseph, what does it say about her disposition at the time of the Annunciation? She certainly was not going to spring this on Joseph as a little surprise when he took her into his home. She waited in the darkness of faith for God to reveal the divine will to her. What do you think Mary felt when the angel left her?

To make the reflection more personal, I suggest some further questions that you might like to consider. Remember that there are no right and wrong answers, and this is not an exam. Do not worry if you take a long time over one question or cannot answer another. The important thing is to listen to what God might be saying to you through this text of Scripture.

1. How does God communicate with you?
2. What do you think God is saying to you?
3. What is your part in God's plan?
4. How can you co-operate more fully with God?

Respond

The purpose of all prayer is to encourage a personal response to God, who always takes the initiative. Having expended some thought on the text, and on what God might be saying to you through it, now is the time to open your heart and communicate directly with the One who loves you beyond anything you could imagine. The prayer below might help you get started, but if you do not need it, even better.

> *Rejoice, you by whom joy will shine forth!*
> *Rejoice, you by whom malediction will cease!*
> *Rejoice, you who raise up the fallen Adam!*
> *Rejoice, you who dry the tears of Eve!*
> *Rejoice, you who are the inaccessible summit of human thought!*
> *Rejoice, you the impenetrable abyss even for the eyes of angels!*
> *Rejoice, because you are the throne of the great King!*
> *Rejoice, for you are the one who bears all things!*
> *Rejoice, announcing star of the sun!*
> *Rejoice, womb of the divine incarnation!*

Rejoice, you by whom creation is renewed!
Rejoice, you by whom and in whom the Creator is adored![19]

Rest

The mission of Jesus was to open the way for human beings to share in the life of God (*2 Peter* 1:4). There is also the startling statement of the great defender of Christian truth, Saint Athanasius (296-373): "For the Son of God became man so that we might become God".[20] Mary's vocation was to co-operate with God in this great work. She joyfully accepted her role, even though she could not foresee where it would lead her. Each of us has a unique vocation to become the child of God that we have been created to be. In our human uniqueness, God expresses the divine presence in an unrepeatable way. This is possible because the Son of God came into the world as one of us, to raise us up to participate in God's life.

The Christian contemplative tradition was largely ignored for several hundred years, for a number of historical reasons, but has recently undergone a resurgence of interest. More and more people are seeking to tune in to the presence of God, which is the ground of all being. New contemplative prayer groups are being founded, and many books are being written to help people deepen their relationship with God. Contemplation is not a technique to be learned; it is a gift to be received. However, there are ways to prepare the soil to receive the seed so that it produces a hundredfold (cf. *Mark* 4:8, 20; *Luke* 8:8). John the Baptist was sent to prepare the way of the Lord, and there are things that we can do as we wait for God. The gift of contemplation is not reserved for holy people, but normally it is facilitated if the individual is in fact seeking God. By 'seeking God' I do not mean looking for something outside, but expressing a desire to be in union with God. The words of Our Lady at the end of the Annunciation scene can express well this desire: "May it be to me as you have said" (*Luke* 1:38). This is not a passive resignation to the will of someone more powerful; it is the joyful cry of co-operation in the great work that God wishes to accomplish in and through her.

God desires to bring about a wonderful work in you. You can ignore this vocation, or fight it, or deny it, or you can joyfully co-operate with God. If you choose to co-operate with God, you will normally begin by putting your house

---

19 A part of the 6th- or 7th-century Greek hymn, the *Akathiste*, composed originally for the feast of the Annunciation.

20 See article 460 in the 1992 *Catechism of the Catholic Church* (London: Geoffrey Chapman / Rome: Libreria Editrice Vaticana, and subsequent publishers) for this and other similar quotes.

in order a little, in the sense that you will turn away from anything that is clearly against God's will. You will have spent some time in trying to discover more and more about God from the Scriptures. You will also normally seek to spend time in prayer, which is the way to grow in your relationship with God. Prayer is a relationship with God and is an intensely personal journey. However, just as there are various guidelines for human relationships, there are also similar guidelines for the human/divine relationship. It is unlikely that you will have a very successful human relationship if you talk all the time, and do not give the other person an opportunity to speak. Also in the relationship with God there is a time for talking and a time for silence.

Silence can be difficult, especially for modern men and women, and so the ways of Christian prayer that are being taught nowadays focus very much on how to remain in silence. Most of these ways of prayer have strong roots in the Christian contemplative tradition, and seek to make known the riches contained there, but they also introduce some elements aimed at the situation in which we find ourselves today. A recent book on the practice of contemplation seeks to teach some skills "by which we learn to dispose ourselves to surrender and thus to discover this uncharted land".[21] The author writes about the use of a prayer word or phrase to help the mind remain in the presence of God rather than flitting about all over the place.

Perhaps there is a word or a phrase that comes to you from your own relationship with God that might help you. If not, I suggest using "Lord", or "Father", or "Jesus", or "Spirit". There are various ways that one can use a prayer word. I prefer to use it in order to refocus the heart when you find yourself wandering. It can remind you of your intention, which is to be in God's presence. Enter into a period of silence now and see whether your prayer word helps you to remain with your heart fixed on God. Let this prayer word bring you back to God when you are following other thoughts.

Act

Throughout your day be aware that God may be communicating with you in the small events. Seek to co-operate with God's plan of salvation for humanity in the humdrum of your life.

---

21 Martin Laird, O.S.A., *Into The Silent Land: The Christian Practice of Contemplation*, (London: Darton, Longman & Todd, 2006), p. 3.

The Visitation, painted by Edward Ardizzone,
at the Church of Our Lady of Mount Carmel in Faversham, Kent, England.

THE MEETING OF MARY AND ELIZABETH
Luke 1:39-45

Opening Prayer

Gracious and loving God, you called Mary and Elizabeth to carry out your plan of salvation by bearing Jesus and John the Baptist for the life of the world. Open the depths of your Word to me and give me the grace to believe in your promises. I make this prayer through Christ Our Lord. Amen.

Text

Read attentively the following Bible text for the first time in order to get an idea of the overall sense and to take in the details. The *New Living Translation* (*NLT*) used for the passage below was an attempt to create a text that would make the same impact on modern readers that the original text had on the first hearers and readers.[22] The translators tried to put the original into everyday English.

> [39] A few days later Mary hurried to the hill country of Judea, to the town [40] where Zechariah lived. She entered the house and greeted Elizabeth. [41] At the sound of Mary's greeting, Elizabeth's child leaped within her, and Elizabeth was filled with the Holy Spirit. [42] Elizabeth gave a glad cry and exclaimed to Mary, "You are blessed by God above all other women, and your child is blessed. [43] What an honor this is, that the mother of my Lord should visit me! [44] When you came in and greeted me, my baby jumped for joy the instant I heard your voice! [45] You are blessed, because you believed that the Lord would do what he said.

Read

This is another favourite topic for some of the greatest painters in the world. It is commonly called 'The Visitation'. Luke began his Gospel with two separate stories of angelic announcements. Now the two stories merge as Mary visits

---

Elizabeth. Why do you think that Mary went to Elizabeth? The angel Gabriel had announced to Zechariah that his son would be filled with the Holy Spirit even from his mother's womb (1:15) and when Elizabeth heard Mary's greeting, the baby leaped for joy in his mother's womb as a fulfilment of the angel's words.

We are told that Elizabeth is filled with the Holy Spirit, which should alert us that her words will be a prophetic utterance. She declares that Mary is blessed because she believed. Like all of the New Testament, Luke recounts his story in the light of the resurrection of Christ, and so he has Elizabeth call Mary, "the mother of my Lord", which is a Christian confession of faith.

Running right through this story is an Old Testament background. The Ark of the Covenant was the symbol of God's presence among the people of the Old Testament; Mary is presented by Luke as the Ark of the New Covenant as she carries within her the presence of God's Son who has come to save the people.

Reflect

Read again the text of *Luke* 1:39-45.

What is going on in this story? Why do you think it was included in Luke's Gospel? What is the main point? Below I suggest some questions in order to help you interiorise the Word of God and apply it to your own life. Perhaps you have other more appropriate questions that might bring this text into the nitty-gritty of your life.

1. Do you hurry to help other people when you become aware of a need?
2. When you help other people, is it for your benefit or theirs?
3. Elizabeth was honoured at Mary's visit. What would make you feel honoured?
4. Do you believe that the Lord will do as he said?
5. What part do you think you have in God's plan?

Respond

Now is the time to let your heart communicate directly with God. Perhaps the prayer below might help you to get started.

> *Almighty, ever-living God,*
> *you inspired the Blessed Virgin Mary,*
> *when she was carrying your Son,*
> *to visit Elizabeth.*

*Grant that, always docile to the voice of the Spirit,
we may, together with Our Lady, glorify your Name.
We make our prayer through our Lord Jesus Christ
your Son, who lives and reigns with you,
in the unity of the Holy Spirit,
one God, forever and ever. Amen.*[23]

Rest

Immediately after the revelation of God, Mary sets out on the long journey to visit her cousin Elizabeth. She goes to help her prepare for the birth of her child and Elizabeth recognises in her the presence of the Lord. The acid test of any religious experience is whether there is some practical fruit emerging from it. If the supposed religious experience makes us more self-centred, it is not from God. If, on the other hand, we become a little more solicitous of the needs of others and forgetful of our own, that is a positive sign. There is no absolute certainty as to whether some experience is from God or not, but it is more likely when there is good fruit.

There has been an upsurge of interest in contemplative prayer in recent years and this has had many positive effects. Of course it is essential to remember that contemplation is a gift from God, and not something that we can manufacture by our own clever techniques. Contemplation, or contemplative prayer, has been defined or described in a variety of ways:

> *The development of one's relationship with Christ to the point of communing beyond words, thoughts, feelings, and the multiplication of particular acts; a process moving from the simplified activity of waiting upon God to the ever-increasing predominance of the Gifts of the Spirit as the source of one's prayer.*[24]

> *In essence, contemplative prayer is simply a wordless trusting openness of self to the divine presence. Far from being advanced, it is about the simplest form of prayer there is.*[25]

> *(Contemplation) is a transforming experience of the overpowering love of God. This love empties us of our limited and imperfect*

23 Conclusion of Morning Prayer on the Feast of the Visitation, 31st May, in *The Divine Office*, (London & Glasgow: Collins, 1974), Vol. III, p. 27*.
24 Thomas Keating, O.C.S.O., *Open Mind, Open Heart*, (Massachusetts: Element Books, 1992), p. 146.
25 Cynthia Bourgeault, *Centering Prayer and Inner Awakening*, (Cambridge, Massachusetts: Cowley Publications, 2004), p. 5.

human ways of thinking, loving and behaving, transforming them into divine ways.[26]

Contemplation is none other than a secret, peaceful and loving infusion of God, which if the soul allows it to happen, enflames it in the spirit of love.[27] Secret contemplation ... is a science of love ... which is an infused loving knowledge that both illuminates and enamours the soul, elevating it step by step unto God its Creator.[28]

Contemplative prayer is the simplest expression of the mystery of prayer. It is a gift, a grace; it can be accepted only in humility and poverty. Contemplative prayer is a covenant relationship established by God within our hearts. Contemplative prayer is a communion in which the Holy Trinity conforms man, the image of God, "to his likeness".[29]

So contemplative prayer, or contemplation, is something God does in those who are willing to receive this gift. Often writers and speakers will use these terms for some form of silent prayer that we can do. I believe this to be mistaken and can lead us astray. What we can do is to prepare for this gift. To use an analogy, if you want to catch the number 9 bus you cannot force the bus to arrive when you want it, but you can make sure you stand in readiness at the number 9 bus-stop; do not complain that your bus never comes if you are waiting at another stop. The different forms of silent prayer that are taught in our days can be very beneficial, and can prepare us for the inflow of God, but they do not make us contemplatives. God makes us contemplatives.

Mary was blessed because she believed that God would accomplish what had been promised. Go before God in faith. This is the time to lay aside your own ideas, thoughts and words, and simply be there with your desire that God transform your heart. When you find that your mind and heart are engaged in distractions, gently remind yourself that you are in the presence of the One who loves you beyond all your imaginings. Do not start thinking about this, but simply be in God's presence to receive what God wishes to give you and say to you at this moment.

---

26 Paragraph 17 of the 1995 *Constitutions of the Carmelite Order*, reproduced in Kevin Alban, O.Carm., (ed.), *Journeying with Carmel*, (Middle Park, Australia: Carmelite Communications, 1997), pp. 14-15.
27 Saint John of the Cross, *Dark Night*, I.10.6.
28 *Ibid.*, 2.18.5.
29 1992 *Catechism of the Catholic Church*, article 2713 (but see the whole section 2712-2719).

Act

If our prayer is truly a communication with God, it will somehow change us. Prayer has an effect on our lives even if we are not aware of it. How are you going to make your prayer a reality in the ordinary events of your life? From the text that you have been considering perhaps you feel moved to do something particular. How about going to the assistance of someone you know needs help? Please do not be like the scout who insisted on helping an old lady across the road even thought she did not want to go! Make sure that your assistance is required and wanted.

Elizabeth was honoured at the visit of the mother of her Lord. You are already filled with the presence of the Lord. Try to be aware today of this constant presence within you in the midst of all your activities.

The Virgin of the Assumption, at Aylesford Carmelite Priory, Kent, England.

REFLECTION 8

MARY PRAISES GOD
Luke 1:46-56

Opening Prayer

O Lord, I give thanks for the wonderful things you are doing within me, even though often your work is hidden. Thank you for your plan of salvation that you are working out in the slow movement of history. Help me to be open to your Word, and filled with the Holy Spirit, to rejoice with the Blessed Virgin Mary now and forever. Amen.

Text

Read attentively the following Bible text for the first time in order to get an idea of the overall sense and to take in the details. You may know this piece of Scripture very well and, if so, you could be surprised at the translation, because it is not quite as you remembered it. This is a very new and fresh translation by the Jesuit Bible scholar Nicholas King, who strives to keep as close as possible to the original Greek.[30] This sometimes means that the style can appear to be rather awkward, but in this way it can draw attention to words or phrases that have become commonplace and so have tended to lose their power. At times it is good to be comforted by the familiar, but it can also be good to be disturbed by the unfamiliar.

> [46] And Mary said, "My soul extols the Lord [47] and my spirit has exulted in God my Saviour [48] because he has looked (favourably) on the humble estate of his slave girl. For look! From now on, all generations will congratulate me [49] because the Powerful One has done great things for me, and holy is his name. [50] And his mercy is for generation after generation on those who fear him. [51] He has done a mighty deed with his arm. He has scattered those who are haughty in the thoughts of their heart. [52] He has deposed rulers from their thrones, and raised up the humble. [53] The hungry he has filled with good things, and the wealthy he has sent away empty. [54]

---

30 *The New Testament, freshly translated by Nicholas King*, (Suffolk: Kevin Mayhew Ltd., 2004), reproduced with permission. I have added the verse numbers.

He has helped his servant Israel, remembering his mercy. [55] As he spoke to our ancestors, to Abraham and his descendants for ever." [56] Mary remained with her about three months, and she returned to her home.

Read

This scene is commonly called 'the Magnificat' from the first word in Latin of Mary's song of praise. It owes much of its inspiration to the Old Testament song of Hannah in *1 Samuel* 2:1-10. The words of praise speak of God's redeeming work, not in the future but as already having been accomplished. This is the confidence of faith. The dramatic reversal of the human norm has come about not by violent revolution but in the humility of Mary through whom will be born the Son of the Most High. He will not come as a mighty warrior but as a little baby.

Luke has already presented Mary as the servant of the Lord (1:38) and now he rejoices in the fruit of her faith and her humility before God. The miracle that God has accomplished by making fruitful Mary's virginity fills all with hope that the divine promises to Israel are now being fulfilled. God is almighty, but exercises this power by coming to the aid of the poor and humble. The proud place themselves outside the salvific plan of God. Mary recognises the wonderful things that God has done in her, and in the history of the people. The guarantee of what God will do in the future is based on what God has already done. The hope of a new world is put before us, in which the usual ways of our world are turned upside-down. The ones who carry forward God's plan are not the proud or the rich, but the poor and those who put their trust in God.

The Magnificat is the prayer of the poor who wait in joyful hope with Mary, the servant of the Lord, for the fulfilment of God's plan of salvation.

Reflect

Read again the text of *Luke* 1:46-56.

What can this very well-known text mean in the concrete reality of my daily life? The new translation may have brought something to your attention that you had not noticed before. It is not sufficient to listen to Scripture with the head; we have to engage the whole of our being in this intimate dialogue with God. Below I suggest some questions to assist the movement of the Word of God from the head to the heart. Perhaps other questions arise in your mind from your reading of the text. This moment is not an intellectual reflection on the meaning of the text in a way that keeps it from influencing us. Instead, the reflection in the movement of *Lectio Divina* is intended to touch our lives, and move on the process of transformation.

1. What do you think God is doing in the modern world?
2. How is God acting in your own life?
3. How do you co-operate with God?
4. What does it mean to be humble before God?

Respond

The following prayer of Hannah in the Old Testament might help you formulate your own prayer. Words, however, are not always the best means of communication. Let your heart speak to God.

1 Samuel 2:1-10 (The New Living Translation)[31]

[1] Then Hannah prayed: "My heart rejoices in the LORD! Oh, how the LORD has blessed me! Now I have an answer for my enemies, as I delight in your deliverance. [2] No one is holy like the LORD! There is no one besides you; there is no Rock like our God. [3] "Stop acting so proud and haughty! Don't speak with such arrogance! The LORD is a God who knows your deeds; and he will judge you for what you have done. [4] Those who were mighty are mighty no more; and those who were weak are now strong. [5] Those who were well fed are now starving; and those who were starving are now full. The barren woman now has seven children; but the woman with many children will have no more. [6] The LORD brings both death and life; he brings some down to the grave but raises others up. [7] The LORD makes one poor and another rich; he brings one down and lifts another up. [8] He lifts the poor from the dust – yes, from a pile of ashes! He treats them like princes, placing them in seats of honor. "For all the earth is the LORD's, and he has set the world in order. [9] He will protect his godly ones, but the wicked will perish in darkness. No one will succeed by strength alone. [10] Those who fight against the LORD will be broken. He thunders against them from heaven; the LORD judges throughout the earth. He gives mighty strength to his king; he increases the might of his anointed one."

---

31 See reflection 7 above.

Rest

The Magnificat is a very rich text that one can approach in various ways. One striking thing is the declaration that God has turned round the normal ways of the world, and that already "He has scattered those who are haughty in the thoughts of their heart. He has deposed rulers from their thrones, and raised up the humble. The hungry he has filled with good things, and the wealthy he has sent away empty." (1:51-53) The contemplative path is a way of faith. It is not cosy but calls into question our motives for believing in God and for trying to do God's will.

The image of journey has often been used when discussing contemplation. Of course we do not have to go far to meet God because, wherever we go, God is there before us. *Psalm* 139 reminds us that God knows us intimately and knows all our ways. Even if we are covered in darkness, it is not dark to God who remains with us. The contemplative path is a journey inwards, but on this path we meet some obstacles that emerge from our own interior life. At the beginning of *The Ascent of Mount Carmel* by Saint John of the Cross, the great Carmelite mystic, he points out that some people resemble children who kick and cry, and struggle to walk by themselves instead of allowing their mothers to carry them; they advance very slowly.[32] They have a lot to learn, and the learning process can be very painful, because through it they begin to see themselves as they are, instead of how they think they are.

The 'false self' is the name given by many to the way human beings seek happiness in ways that can never fully satisfy.[33] We all want to be happy, and we are programmed to seek happiness. Human beings are made for God, and only God can fill "the deep caverns of feeling".[34] Unfortunately, our tendency is to seek the fulfilment that only God can give in ways that can never satisfy. We believe that we will be fully satisfied if we can control our little world, if we are receiving the affection that we believe is our due, and if our basic survival is guaranteed. Of course, the more we have, the more we seek, and our demands become impossible to be satisfied. Our tendency is to turn anything into an idol, that is, we seek from people and objects the enduring happiness that can come only from God.

---

32   Saint John of the Cross, *Ascent of Mount Carmel*, Prologue, 3.
33   For a fuller explanation of the false self, see Thomas Keating, *Invitation to Love*, (Dorset: Element Books Ltd., 1992) and Elizabeth Smith & Joseph Chalmers, *A Deeper Love* (London & New York: Continuum, 1999).
34   Cf. Saint John of the Cross, *The Living Flame*, Stanza 3.

The 'false self' will seek even to use God and religion for selfish purposes. This is one reason why religion itself is sometimes accused of being a menace to humanity! People will use anything, including religion, to fulfil what they perceive to be their needs. Religion, of course, is intended to lead us to God. All the world religions, as far as I know, speak of peace and love and so on. Perhaps the present situation in western countries of aggressive secularism trying to ridicule religion and marginalise it will actually prove to be a great blessing, as religion will not be as 'useful' to the 'false self' as in the past. The decision to follow the still small voice of God, who calls us to enter on the path to eternal life, is a very personal – and sometimes courageous – decision, without many of the usual social supports of the past.

When we actually begin to seek God seriously, and not just play at being religious, we enter more deeply into the relationship with God who is determined to bring us to the fullness of life. This fullness requires the death of the 'false self', which is not accomplished overnight, but rather takes at least a lifetime of responding to the grace of God. At all times we have to be on the lookout for the 'false self' poking its nose into our affairs. When we begin to take the relationship with God seriously, we naturally turn to prayer in some form. Prayer is the relationship with God, and so there are innumerable ways to respond to God's initiative. Any prayer that is an opening to God is good. At different times on our journey, different ways of prayer will suit more than others. The Eucharist and the Divine Office are the prayer of Christ, and sharing with other people in this prayer is always important on the journey, but at some points it will seem more meaningful than at others. The liturgy is always meaningful, but at times our ability to appreciate its depths is not as great as at other times. Reciting the vocal prayers many of us learned as children often remains a staple of our relationship with God, but the balance of this way of prayer and other, more silent, ways changes as we grow in our relationship with God. We do normally have to spend some time thinking about God, and about the various aspects of our faith, so that the relationship with God does not remain superficial. We can see many examples in the Gospels where Jesus challenged his disciples to grow in their faith. God challenges us; if we fail to respond, we cannot hope for a deep relationship. There does come a time in every relationship when words become less important, and a different way of responding is required. Words can become less important and silence more meaningful.

There are several ways of prayer that help people when they feel called to more and more silence. These ways do not suit everyone, and they are not better than any other ways of prayer. Different ways of prayer will respond to our needs at specific times of our lives, and we should remain flexible. The 'false self' can intrude here and grasp hold of some way of prayer for its own purposes. If a particular style of prayer helps you to feel good or to feel superior, beware! The purpose of prayer is to open us to a relationship with God; the 'false self' will grasp hold of something far less.

Ask God to lead you to a way of prayer that will help you grow spiritually, and in how you relate to other people and the world around you. Wait, with Mary, in the silence, for God to stir your heart.

Act

Prayer is the expression of the relationship with God, but the 'false self' is quite happy to say prayers if it can use that activity to boost its own low self-esteem and insecurity. The way to be sure that your prayer is authentic, that is, is an in-depth communication with God, is that it positively affects your ordinary life. Try to translate your prayer into life now. Thank God for the significant people in your life, and for those who cross your path today. Can you be pleasant to those you meet? Try to tune into God's action in the world around you – in nature and events as well as in people.

The nativity, after a painting by Adam Kossowski,
at the Church of Our Lady of Mount Carmel, Faversham, Kent, England.

MARY AND THE BIRTH OF JESUS
Luke 2:1-20

Opening Prayer

O Lord, you guide the course of world events in order to further your plan of salvation for humanity. Help me to be aware of your presence and action through history, and in my own life. May your Word continue to bear abundant fruit, and may it be the source of eternal life for all. Through Christ Our Lord. Amen.

Text

Read attentively the following Bible text for the first time in order to get an idea of the overall sense and to take in the details. The original idea behind the translation from which our passage below is taken – the *Good News Bible* (*GNB*) – was that it be easily understandable by all, non-native English speakers and children alike.[35] It began life in the United States of America as the *Good News Translation*. It is a very popular version of the Bible.

[1] At that time the Emperor Augustus ordered a census to be taken throughout the Roman Empire. [2] When this first census took place Quirinius was the governor of Syria. [3] Everyone, then, went to register himself, each to his own town. [4] Joseph went from the town of Nazareth in Galilee to the town of Bethlehem in Judea, the birthplace of King David. Joseph went there because he was a descendant of David. [5] He went to register with Mary who was promised in marriage to him. She was pregnant [6] and while they were in Bethlehem the time came for her to have her baby. [7] She gave birth to her first son, wrapped him in strips of cloth and laid him in a manger – there was no room for them to stay in the inn. [8] There were some shepherds in that part of the country who were spending the night in the fields, taking care of their flocks. [9] An angel of the Lord appeared to them, and the glory of the Lord shone

---

over them. They were terribly afraid [10] but the angel said to them, "Don't be afraid! I am here with good news for you, which will bring great joy to all the people. [11] This very day in David's town your saviour was born – Christ the Lord! [12] And this is what will prove it to you: you will find a baby wrapped in strips of cloth and lying in a manger." [13] Suddenly a great army of heaven's angels appeared with the angel singing praises to God: [14] "Glory to God in the highest heaven, and peace on earth to those with whom he is pleased!" [15] When the angels went away from them back into heaven, the shepherds said to one another, "Let's go to Bethlehem and see this thing that has happened, which the Lord has told us." [16] So they hurried off and found Mary and Joseph and found the baby lying in the manger. [17] When the shepherds saw him they told them what the angel had said about the child. [18] All who heard it were amazed at what the shepherds said. [19] Mary remembered all these things and thought deeply about them. [20] The shepherds went back, singing praises to God for all they had heard and seen; it had been just as the angel had told them.

Read

There are a number of historical difficulties regarding the census. It has been suggested that Luke was confused about some of the details. While this is possible, there is also another thing to consider. Luke may have recounted the story of the birth of Jesus in the context of the census called by the Roman Emperor in order to make a point about Christ. The Emperor was often acclaimed as the bringer of peace, even though he had done so by his conquering armies. Perhaps Luke wanted to make clear that in fact it is God who is the bringer of peace, and God does so in the midst of human events and in very humble ways. It is very easy to miss God's activity. The census also allowed Luke to explain why Jesus of Nazareth actually came to be born in Bethlehem, the town of King David. Nazareth was completely insignificant, but Bethlehem was mentioned several times in the Bible, and some expected the Messiah to come from there.

The title "Son of David" is used three times for Jesus in Luke's Gospel (18:38, 39; 20:41). This was a title for the long-awaited Messiah of Israel, and Luke establishes Jesus' connections to David from the very beginning.

Luke was writing a gospel and not a history textbook. We should not get too hung up about the historical details; instead, we should ask what is Luke saying about Jesus and Mary – and us – by means of the details? The details of the birth are very spare. Jesus is Mary's firstborn. This does not mean that Mary had other children but is a common term in the Bible to indicate the one who will carry on the family line, and it could be a reference to the importance of the firstborn being consecrated to God.

Matthew tells us that wise men came from the east and paid homage to Jesus. Luke, on the other hand, tells us that the birth was announced to shepherds. These people were despised in the first century, even though the great King David had himself been a shepherd. Perhaps Luke is once again stressing the connections between Jesus and King David, as well as making it clear that Jesus came to the poor, a recurrent theme in the rest of the Gospel. In one short story we move from the Emperor Augustus and end with poor shepherds. The angels announce to the shepherds the birth of the long-awaited Messiah.

We are told that Mary "remembered all these things and thought deeply about them". She is the servant of the Lord, and very carefully ponders on everything that happens, so as not to miss what God is saying.

Reflect

Read again the text of *Luke* 2:1-20.

What does this Word mean to you? It is a mistake to get so caught up in the details of the story, and in the scenes that your imagination may weave, that you miss the main point. It really does not matter if each detail actually happened. What is important is Luke's point that the birth of Christ in obscurity is a pivotal moment in the history of the world. This is Good News from God, especially to the poor. Like Mary, we need to ponder what God has done and is doing, so that we can be open to receive what God wants to give us.

The questions below are intended to help you to interiorise the Word of God and open your daily life to God's purifying and transforming action.

1. What is the most important point for you of the story of Jesus' birth?
2. The angels announced the birth of Christ the Lord. What does that mean for you?
3. Mary remembered all these things and thought deeply about them. Remember when the activity of God in your life was particularly clear. What is God doing in your life now?

Respond

We can easily spend a lot of time in our heads, and not allow what we are pondering to really affect our lives. This is the moment in the movement of *Lectio Divina* to engage the heart. Let your heart communicate with God in your own way. The prayer below may help you to get started.

> *Almighty God, who chose the blessed Virgin Mary to be the mother of your only Son: grant that we who are redeemed by his blood may share with her in the glory of your eternal kingdom; through Jesus Christ our Lord, who is alive and reigns with you and the Holy Spirit, one God, now and for ever. Amen.*[36]

Rest

God's ways are not our ways. Mary thought deeply about everything that took place in order to discover what God was saying. When we are seeking God's will we must not ignore the obvious. We have the commandments, and the teaching and example of Jesus. However, there are times when things are not so obvious. In our reading, the shepherds heard about the birth of the Messiah from a choir of heavenly angels. Usually we do not receive messages like that, and we have to walk by faith, which is dark in the sense that what we believe may not be the most obvious thing. The Carmelite Saint John of the Cross writes beautifully about the 'dark night' as a metaphor for the inevitable sense of loss that the individual pray-er experiences as he or she matures. It is a law of human development that we have to leave behind many stages in order to grow up. It is tragic to meet someone who is an adult but whose emotional responses are more suited to a child. Normally we learn from the experience of life what is appropriate and what is not. In the relationship with God, the believer has to grow up, and in doing so leave behind a childish way of relating. The Gospel command to be childlike is not the same as being childish. We have to learn to relate as adult children of God.

It can be hard to leave behind ways or things that gave us some security. If other things do not take their place immediately, the individual will go through a process that is akin to mourning. Contemplative prayer is something that God does in us, and not something we can do. However, it seems that God often responds when we show that we are in earnest. Of course, as soon as you think you have God sussed, things will not happen the way you think! In the

---

36 From the *Alternative Service Book*, (Clowes / S.P.C.K. / Cambridge University Press, 1980), pp. 796-97.

analogy we used in reflection 7, we can only wait at the number 9 bus-stop. Perhaps we will have to wait there a very long time, or perhaps the bus will come very quickly. God may call us to greater silence, and may waken gently within us, as it were. At first, the presence of God will be so gentle as to be virtually imperceptible. Our awareness of God's presence and action within us may grow or may not. That is not really important. What is important is that we respond in whatever way we can to what we believe God is doing within us.

The first period of spiritual darkness is normally experienced by people who have thrown themselves with fervour into the relationship with God. They can be like new converts for whom everything is new and fresh. The liturgy, saying prayers, and reading spiritual books can give real pleasure, but there will come a time when the pleasure decreases and eventually dies out. We can wonder what has happened when our usual devotions do not give us the kick they used to. The baby has to be weaned off milk at some time in order to appreciate the culinary delights of haggis or other such delicacies! However, I do admit that perhaps haggis might take some time to get used to. The time it takes to get used to haggis, or a new way of relating to God, can be difficult in different measures. We can regret the passing of a way of prayer that gave us satisfaction in the past but no longer does so. It can seem that God has left us. This is not true; it is simply that God is calling us deeper, but it may not seem so at the time. There is an intensification of God's self-communication, and at first this causes darkness.

The term 'dark night' is bandied around a great deal, and has been expanded to cover the experience of whole societies, and indeed of the whole world. However, in the understanding of John of the Cross, there is quite a specific meaning, and there are signs that it is indeed the 'dark night' and not some other spiritual problem.[37] Firstly, the individual can no longer use his or her mind at the time of prayer to reflect on God. It just becomes impossible. However, alone this could have other causes. Secondly, the enthusiasm goes out of the person who is entering the first period of the 'dark night'. However, this too could have other causes. The clincher is the third sign: that the person, despite everything, is deeply committed to seeking God in prayer and desires to be faithful to Jesus Christ in daily life. When these three signs come together, it is a sign that the person should not worry but have confidence that God really is at work. The 'dark night' is a time of transition to a new way of prayer, and a new way of receiving God.

---

37 Cf. John of the Cross, *Ascent of Mount Carmel*, II.13.2-4 and *Dark Night*, I.9.

When we no longer receive satisfaction from our devotions, it can be hard to remain faithful to the daily encounter with God in prayer. A prayer-word that sums up your desire for God can be like an arrow that pierces the 'cloud of unknowing'.[38] Choose a word that is meaningful for you in your relationship with God; let it communicate your desire for God, even though you may feel very far away. Let your word arise within you whenever you become aware of being distracted.

Act

What is the use of prayer? It is the response to God's initiative, who seeks to establish a relationship with each one of us. Each relationship is unique, and some are more distant than others. You cannot judge any relationship only on how you feel. You must look at the whole reality. You certainly cannot judge your relationship with God on how you feel, as feelings can change with the weather. The only way to get an idea whether or not your relationship with God is developing in a healthy way is to look at the whole of your life. Are you growing, or are you stuck?

Try to apply your prayer today to your daily life. Angels appeared in the story of Jesus' birth. The meaning of the word "angel" is a messenger from God. Be on the lookout today for God's messengers, who can come to us looking like very ordinary people. What is God saying to you today in the midst of your daily activities, and how will you respond?

---

[38] See the way of prayer in the famous book, *Cloud of Unknowing and Other Works,* translated by Clifton Wolters, (London: Penguin Books, 1961).

*The presentation of Jesus at the Temple (the purification of Mary)
depicted in the 'Reconstructed Carmelite Missal' owned by the Carmelite friars in
London c.1380, and now in the British Library, London,
Ms. Additional 29704-5, folio 93r.*

3

MARY WITH THE CHILD JESUS IN THE TEMPLE
Luke 2:22-33

Opening Prayer

Loving God, you inspired Mary and Joseph to present Jesus in the Temple. Simeon saw in the little child the fulfilment of all the promises in the Scriptures. Help me to be open to your Word, and to rejoice in the revelation of your salvation. Through Christ Our Lord. Amen.

Text

Read attentively the following Scripture text for the first time in order to get an idea of the overall sense and to take in the details. The passage is taken from a translation called *The World English Bible*, an update of the *American Standard Version* of 1901.[39]

> [22] When the days of their purification according to the law of Moses were fulfilled, they brought him up to Jerusalem, to present him to the Lord [23] (as it is written in the law of the Lord, "Every male who opens the womb shall be called holy to the Lord") [24] and to offer a sacrifice according to that which is said in the law of the Lord, "A pair of turtledoves, or two young pigeons." [25] Behold, there was a man in Jerusalem whose name was Simeon. This man was righteous and devout, looking for the consolation of Israel, and the Holy Spirit was on him. [26] It had been revealed to him by the Holy Spirit that he should not see death before he had seen the Lord's Christ. [27] He came in the Spirit into the temple. When the parents brought in the child, Jesus, that they might do concerning him according to the custom of the law, [28] then he received him into his arms, and blessed God, and said, [29] "Now you are releasing your servant, Master, according to your word, in peace; [30] for my eyes have seen your salvation, [31] which you have prepared before

---

39 *The World English Bible*, (Rainbow Missions, 2000). This is a modern version of the Bible in the public domain (not subject to copyright) and can be found on the internet at www.ebible.org. The editing of the whole of Scripture has not been finished by the *World English Bible* project, but the New Testament is ready.

the face of all peoples; [32] a light for revelation to the nations, and the glory of your people Israel." [33] Joseph and his mother were marvelling at the things which were spoken concerning him.

Read

The point of all the details in this story is to present the Good News of who Jesus is, and what he will do in the future. Mary and Joseph obeyed God's Law in everything. New parents had some important things to do in order to fulfil what the Law required. They had the baby circumcised on the eighth day (2:21). This was the sign for male children of being members of the Chosen People (*Genesis* 17:10, 13). Normally this ceremony took place in a synagogue or the Temple before witnesses. There was one official witness, and another seat for the Prophet Elijah, who was considered to be spiritually present at the event. Circumcision became an important spiritual occasion and there was a tendency to speak also of 'circumcision of the heart' (*Leviticus* 26:41; *Jeremiah* 4:4; *Romans* 2:28-29), meaning conversion of the heart to God. The sign of the covenant with God must not only be carried on the body but must also be interior. The mother had also to undergo the ceremony of purification, and the parents redeemed their first born (*Exodus* 13:13; *Numbers* 18:15). As a reminder of the Exodus, the firstborn child was consecrated to the Lord (*Exodus* 13:2, 11-16). The firstborn male was to be redeemed (i.e., bought back) at a price of five shekels of silver (*Numbers* 18:15-16). Luke does not mention this requirement. The other ritual prescribed by the Law was the purification of the mother. After the birth of a male child, the mother was ceremonially unclean for seven days and underwent purification for 33 days; the period was twice as long for a female child (*Leviticus* 12:1-5). During this time, the mother was not permitted to enter the Temple or touch any holy object. After the 40 (or 80) days, she was to offer a lamb and a pigeon or turtledove. If she could not afford a lamb, she could offer instead two turtledoves or pigeons (*Leviticus* 12:6-8). Luke's account of the presentation of Jesus in the Temple stresses the fulfilment of all that the Law required at the birth of a child.

For Simeon, the birth of Jesus is the sign he was waiting for that finally God has sent the Messiah to Israel. He gives thanks to God for sending the Christ as a "light for revelation to the nations", that is, the Gentiles. Luke is stressing here that Jesus is the saviour of all people.

Luke records the reaction of Mary and Joseph. In the translation we are using for this piece of Scripture, it says: "Joseph and his mother". In many translations we find: "his father and mother". Perhaps it was changed by the editors of the *World English Bible* because they did not think it proper to call Joseph the father of Jesus. However, Joseph was indeed the legal father of the child as he had accepted what God wanted of him. Luke has made it abundantly clear by this stage that Jesus is unique, and that his mother was a virgin, and so does not feel the need to hammer home the point.

Reflect

Read again the text of *Luke* 2:22-33. How does this text of Scripture actually affect your life? We read that Joseph and Mary marvelled at the things spoken about him. I want to suggest some questions that are designed to help you to reflect on this passage of Scripture and its connection to your ordinary existence. I invite you to ponder and to allow space for the Word of God to penetrate your heart.

1. Mary and Joseph presented Jesus to the Lord. What can you present?
2. Simeon was happy because he saw in Jesus the fulfilment of all God's promises in Scripture. What does Jesus mean to you?
3. Mary and Joseph marvelled at their part in God's plan of salvation. What do you think God is asking you to do?

Respond

Now is the time to let your heart communicate with God. Perhaps you could ask Mary to help you say to God what is in your heart. The poem below might help get you started.

> *To she who is infinitely queen*
> *Because she is the most humble of creatures.*
> *Because she was a poor woman, a miserable woman,*
> *a poor Jewess from Judea.*
> *To she who is infinitely distant*
> *Because she is infinitely near.*
> *To she who is the highest princess*
> *Because she is the most humble woman.*
> *To she who is the nearest to God*
> *Because she is the nearest to men.*
> *To she who is infinitely saved*
> *Because in her turn she saves infinitely.*[40]

---

40 A poem by Charles Péguy, quoted in Sarah Jane Boss, (ed.), *Mary: The Complete Resource*, (London & New York: Continuum, 2007), p. 529.

Rest

Mary and Joseph were struck by everything that was being said about Jesus when they took him to the Temple in Jerusalem for the first time. Churches are hopefully sacred spaces where the communication with God is encouraged, but God is not confined to places of worship. When we enter a church, hopefully we are willing and ready to listen to what God has to say to us. However, God speaks in many different ways and uses many forms. Often our time of prayer can seem very dry or distracted, and we can think that God has nothing to say to us, but in fact God will communicate with us outside the time of prayer. In order to receive what God wants to give us we must remain on God's wavelength throughout the day. Our time of prayer is an encounter with God, no matter what it feels like. It is this daily meeting with God that tunes us in and makes us sensitive to what God is saying throughout the day. All great sportsmen and women practice a lot; without the arduous practice they would soon lose their touch that makes them that bit special. Without prayer a Christian begins to lose touch with the source of all life, and it becomes more and more difficult to remain open to whatever God desires to communicate.

There are several new prayer forms that are specifically intended to help people be open to receive the gift of contemplation. Perhaps the most popular are 'Centering Prayer' (otherwise known as 'Prayer in Secret'), and 'Christian Meditation'.[41] Both use a prayer word, though in different ways. Christian Meditation uses a mantra, that is, the constant repeating of "ma-ra-na-tha" (Aramaic for "Come Lord"). The mantra is to be recited silently and interiorly with four equally-stressed syllables. Attention is to be given to the sound of the mantra and whenever distractions arise, one is to return to the mantra. Centering Prayer, on the other hand, does not use a mantra but a 'sacred word', that is, a word that is sacred to the individual. The sacred word is not repeated constantly like a mantra, but is used only when you find that you are engaged with any thought, in order to reiterate your intention to consent to the presence and action of God in your life. It is silent and is the symbol of your fundamental intention.

---

41 'Centering Prayer' was formulated originally by three Trappist monks in the U.S.A. The basic book on the subject is by Thomas Keating, O.C.S.O., *Open Mind, Open Heart*, (Massachusetts: Element Books, 1992). Keating has written many books with the same thrust; the latest in which he refines the method is: *Manifesting God* (New York: Lantern Books, 2005). For a simple introduction to this method of prayer, see Elizabeth Smith & Joseph Chalmers, *A Deeper Love* (London & New York: Continuum, 1999). For the use of this method of prayer in the context of *Lectio Divina* see my book *The Sound of Silence*, (Faversham & Rome: Saint Albert's Press & Edizioni Carmelitane, 2007). For up-to-date information on Centering Prayer see the website of *Contemplative Outreach UK*: www.couk.org.uk. John Main, a Benedictine monk, is the pioneer of 'Christian Meditation'. His work has been continued by Laurence Freeman, also a monk. For further information see the website of *The World Community for Christian Meditation*: www.wccm.org.

The teachers of both these forms of silent prayer suggest that it be used twice a day for twenty or thirty minutes each time. However, anything is better than nothing, and only you can decide how much time you can spare. Take some time now to be in God's presence. Perhaps you might like to try one of these prayer forms. If you are interested in taking either a bit further, you could check out the resources referred to in the footnotes where you will find some suggestions.

Act

We communicate in many ways – with words, of course, but also with gestures, looks, sighs, silence and so on. Prayer is the way we communicate with God, who always takes the initiative in this dialogue. There are very many ways to pray, and the more important the relationship with God is to us, the more ways we will utilise. Prayer should not be confined to particular times when we 'say our prayers', but involves the whole of our relationship with God. We will read Scripture as the Word of God, and perhaps some book that helps us grow in our desire for God. We might meet with like-minded people for prayer, using *Lectio Divina* or one of the modern adaptations of ancient methods. Throughout the day, we will remain in conscious contact with God in the midst of our busy daily activities with a word or a sigh or an interior glance. God is the source of all being, and nothing has existence except in the divine stream of life.

Life is so busy that many people seem to be completely unaware, or even consciously reject, that they are held in being moment by moment. Militant secularists want to push religion from the public square into the realm of the purely private. While an intimate relationship should not be trumpeted to the whole world, it still must have an effect on how one lives. It is not necessary to talk about your relationship with God to all and sundry, and indeed that would be a sign of something amiss, but a profound relationship will have a profound effect on how you relate to the world around you. You cannot have a deep relationship with God and treat other people and the environment in a totally selfish way.

Stay in touch with God today in any way you know how, and ask to be enlightened about how you treat the people around you and the world in which you live.

The presentation of the child Jesus in the Temple,
after a painting by Adam Kosskowski
at the Church of Our Lady of Mount Carmel, Faversham, Kent, England.

MARY AND THE PROPHECY
Luke 2:34-40

Opening Prayer

> *O God, you sent your Son to bring life into the world, but he was and continues to be a sign of contradiction. He probes the human heart, and all peoples must stand before him for judgement. A sword pierced the soul of Mary, his Mother, who stood by him. Purify my heart so that I might truly listen to your Word and be transformed by its presence in my life. Through Christ Our Lord. Amen.*

Text

Read attentively the following Bible text for the first time in order to get an idea of the overall sense and to take in the details. The text below is from the *Contemporary English Version* (*CEV*).[42] It is intended to be an accurate and faithful translation that is easily read by children and those whose first language is not English.

> [34] Then he blessed them and told Mary, "This child of yours will cause many people in Israel to fall and others to stand. The child will be like a warning sign. Many people will reject him, [35] and you, Mary, will suffer as though you had been stabbed by a dagger. But all this will show what people are really thinking." [36] The prophet Anna was also there in the temple. She was the daughter of Phanuel from the tribe of Asher, and she was very old. In her youth she had been married for seven years, but her husband had died. [37] And now she was eighty-four years old. Night and day she served God in the temple by praying and often going without eating. [38] At that time Anna came in and praised God. She spoke about the child Jesus to everyone who hoped for Jerusalem to be set free. [39] After Joseph and Mary had done everything that the Law of the Lord commands, they returned home to Nazareth in Galilee. [40] The child Jesus grew. He became strong and wise, and God blessed him.

---

42 *Contemporary English Version* copyright © 1991, 1992, 1995 American Bible Society; used by permission; all rights reserved.

Read

This text is the continuation of the previous one where Mary and Joseph visit the Temple in Jerusalem. Simeon sees the baby and is overjoyed that finally God has fulfilled the promises of the Old Testament by sending the Messiah. However, Simeon prophesies that not everyone will accept Jesus and he "will cause many people in Israel to fall and others to stand". The one who would bring salvation would also bring judgement. Everyone would have to make a decision in his regard. People can accept or reject salvation. Then comes the mysterious prophecy concerning the role of Mary about a sword piercing her soul, or as the contemporary translation has it, "and you, Mary, will suffer as though you had been stabbed by a dagger." The mother of Jesus would share in some way in the pain of the rejection of her son.

The old widow Anna then praises God and speaks about the child to all who were awaiting the fulfilment of God's promises. The hope for Jerusalem to be set free is the same as waiting expectantly for the coming of the Messiah to Israel. For Luke Jerusalem plays a central role in the work of salvation. Then we have the conclusion to the whole of the infancy story by relating that, after having done everything that the Law of God required, they returned home to Nazareth, where Jesus continued to grow as any other child. He was indeed a real human person while at the same time being the Son of God.

Reflect

Read again the text of *Luke* 2:34-40.

Mary and Joseph did all that the Law of God required. Jewish life was, and is, marked by recognition of God in the midst of ordinary events. Until quite recently most Christian cultures had a similar emphasis. In recent times we seem to have lost the immediate remembrance of God in the busyness of daily life. The pressures of secularism and modern life have reduced the significance of ritual in the lives of most Christians. Busy schedules mean that families eat fewer meals together. Family prayer, or even prayer before meals, seems to be a thing of the past in many homes today. For many, religious rituals are reduced to church attendance at Christmas and Easter, and to socially-required ceremonies at births, weddings, and funerals. The marking of both daily and special events with rituals that recognise the sacredness of life and the presence of God in the everyday is practically extinct. The result has been that God has receded from the awareness and experience of everyday life. Many assume that God is found only in certain places, in sacred buildings, in holy books, or in observances led by holy persons. Their lives, on the other hand, move in a secular realm devoid of the presence of the holy. Daily experiences are reduced and impoverished. They have no meaning beyond themselves, no opening to transcendence. Little room for mystery remains in the everyday as it becomes increasingly subject to secularism and technology. What have we lost by removing ritual observances from our daily experience?[43]

The following questions are intended to help you reflect on your own relationship to the transcendent.

1. How can you open your daily existence more to that which is beyond the material?
2. What does your daily life reveal about your true values?
3. Being the mother of Jesus must have brought Mary many joys, but it also brought her great suffering. How does your relationship with Jesus Christ touch your daily life?
4. Anna dedicated her life to God. Where is your heart?

Respond

Reflection can only take us so far, and then the heart takes over. Let your heart speak now to God in whatever way you feel drawn. The poem below might help.

O great Mary, listen to me,
praying to you should be my zeal;
on your brother turn not your back,
Mother of the King of all.

You, Mary, Mother of God,
no-one ever knew your joy,
a royal tree divided in three,
heaven's king was in your womb.

May I be guided by you both
into your good house and your fort,
O great Mary, O my soul,
O golden apple, apple-tree new grown.

---

43 This paragraph is taken from R. Alan Culpepper, 'The Gospel of Luke', in *The New Interpreter's Bible*, (Nashville: Abingdon Press, 1995-2002), Vol. IX, p. 74.

O food, O clothing to dispose,
O tresses rippling as in a field,
O Mother, O Sister, O Love,
your poor brother rightly steer.[44]

Rest

Our previous Bible text ended by telling us that Mary and Joseph marvelled at the wonderful things that were being said about Jesus (2:33). In the continuation of the text we have just reflected on, they are certainly brought down to earth with a bump! Simeon blesses them and turns to Mary saying, "This child of yours will cause many people in Israel to fall and others to stand. The child will be like a warning sign. Many people will reject him, and you, Mary, will suffer as though you had been stabbed by a dagger." (2:34-35).

Saint Luke does not beat about the bush. He tells it like it is. Following Jesus necessarily leads us into conflict. Everyone must make a decision for or against God, and this is done not necessarily in words but in the practical reality of everyday life. He was rejected, and making a fundamental decision for Christ will certainly not guarantee a peaceful life. Problems are part of life, but they can have a positive side by eliciting strength from us that we did not know we possessed.

It should be no surprise that the way of prayer does have its problems. Prayer is a personal relationship with God and any relationship, specially this one, will change us in some way. God is not a comfort-blanket or an instantly obedient hot water tap. God is the Creator of all that is, seen and unseen. Human reason can reach out towards the divine but we could know little of God without the revelation given to us in the history of the Chosen People and above all in Jesus Christ. Throughout the whole of the Bible we can read with amazement that God, who created us, wants to have a relationship with us, but in order to make us capable of receiving the fullness of life we must be prepared. Therefore, God leads us and purifies us. If our prayer does not lead us to consent to God's action in our lives, there is something wrong.

Take some time to be in God's presence, consenting to God's action in your life.

---

44 From Muireadhach Albanach's 13th-century verse *Eistidh Riomsa, A Muire Mhor*, translated by Meg Bateman as *O Great Mary, Listen to Me*, in Meg Bateman, Robert Crawford & James McGonigal, (eds.), *Scottish Religious Poetry: An Anthology*, (Edinburgh: St. Andrew Press, 2000), pp. 34-35.

Act

Let your prayer seep into your daily life. Seek to touch the transcendent beyond but at the heart of all reality. Everything you do has an eternal significance. How can making a cup of tea be a prayer? How can doing the shopping change anything in the sphere of the eternal? A contemplative is in tune with God at all times, whether consciously or not, because he or she has no internal blocks to the divine flow of life. Seek to be aware today of any block in your life. Let your every action and every word be in tune with God.

The finding of the child Jesus in the Temple.
Ceramic by Adam Kossowski in the St. Joseph Chapel at Aylesford Priory, Kent, England.

MARY AND JESUS AT TWELVE YEARS OF AGE
Luke 2:41-51

Opening Prayer

Gracious and Loving God, in your plan of salvation for humanity you sent your only Son into the world as one of us. He grew up under the watchful care of Joseph and Mary, but came to understand that his mission was to the whole world. Let me be open to his message so that, like Mary, I may keep his sayings in my heart. Through Christ Our Lord. Amen.

Text

Read attentively the following Bible text for the first time in order to get an idea of the overall sense and to take in the details. The translation – the *American Standard Version* (*ASV*) of 1901 – is rather old and can sound somewhat archaic.[45] The Jehovah's Witnesses used this version of the Bible for many years until it was supplanted by a new translation.

[41] And his parents went every year to Jerusalem at the feast of the passover. [42] And when he was twelve years old, they went up after the custom of the feast; [43] and when they had fulfilled the days, as they were returning, the boy Jesus tarried behind in Jerusalem; and his parents knew it not; [44] but supposing him to be in the company, they went a day's journey; and they sought for him among their kinsfolk and acquaintance: [45] and when they found him not, they returned to Jerusalem, seeking for him. [46] And it came to pass, after three days they found him in the temple, sitting in the midst of the teachers, both hearing them, and asking them questions: [47] and all that heard him were amazed at his understanding and his answers. [48] And when they saw him, they were astonished; and his mother said unto him, Son, why hast thou thus dealt with us? behold, thy father and I sought thee sorrowing. [49] And he said unto them, How is it that ye sought me? knew ye not that I must be in my Father's house? [50] And they understood not the saying which he spake unto

---

45   The *American Standard Version* is in the public domain and may be read online at: www.ebible.org/asv.

them. [51] And he went down with them, and came to Nazareth; and he was subject unto them: and his mother kept all these sayings in her heart.

Read

Luke is the only Gospel to include a story from Jesus' childhood. Some of the apocryphal gospels have fanciful stories of miracles that the child Jesus performed, but these were never accepted as true Gospels by the Church. This story records Jesus' dawning awareness of who he is and his true relationship to the Father. This story is not a psychological profile of Jesus, nor does it explain Mary's understanding of who her son is. The point of the story is to express a truth about Jesus, that he is the Son of God. Jesus' words to Mary and Joseph are his first recorded words in the Gospel and therefore they are important. These words convey the main point of the story.

The previous scene emphasised that Joseph and Mary carefully observed the Jewish laws. The family's journey to Jerusalem each year for the Passover celebration fulfilled the requirements that all male Israelites should make a pilgrimage to Jerusalem for the feasts of Passover, Pentecost, and Tabernacles (*Exodus* 34:23). Moving at a pace of fifteen miles a day, their journey to Jerusalem would have taken four or five days. According to later Jewish custom, a male child became a man and embraced the traditions of his ancestors at the age of thirteen. At twelve, therefore, Jesus was still a child.[46]

Many commentators have seen in the three days that Jesus was missing an allusion to the three days that he would later spend in the tomb. Verse 49 gives us the words of Jesus. Jesus says that he "must" be in his Father's house. This is a way that the Bible has to express the will of God. Jesus responded to God's will throughout his whole life. His life was not driven by fate or the decisions of others; it was the will of his Father that guided him. The words of Jesus might also mean that he had to be involved in his Father's business. Mary tells Jesus that his father (meaning Joseph) and she sought him "sorrowing". Jesus makes the point that his Father is God. This is not a rejection of Joseph or Mary but a clarification that he does not ultimately belong to them but to God. It is very clear in Luke's Gospel that Joseph is not the physical father of Jesus, but by naming him and accepting him as his son, he became the legal father.

---

46 R. Alan Culpepper, 'The Gospel of Luke', in *The New Interpreter's Bible*, (Nashville: Abingdon Press, 1995-2002), Vol. IX, pp. 76-77.

Luke makes it clear that Jesus kept the fourth commandment of honouring his father and mother by going back with them to Nazareth and being subject to them. Luke presents Mary as responsive to God's will as it is expressed through the events of her life. She kept all these things in her heart. Why do you think that Luke does not say "Mary and Joseph kept all these things in their hearts"?

Reflect

Read again the text of *Luke* 2:41-51.

Have you ever lost something precious? Have you ever lost something that you were keeping for someone else? Losing a child is unimaginable to all but those who have been through the devastating experience. Mary and Joseph had been given the sacred duty of taking care of God's Son and now they had lost him. Added to the normal agony of parents in this situation was the grief that they had failed God.

For twelve years Jesus had acted like a normal child, and perhaps this had lulled Mary and Joseph into a false sense of security. Now at twelve years of age, Jesus reminds them that he came into the world for a particular mission, and that they too have a mission. What is God asking of you? The following questions might or might not be helpful in trying to make this a little clearer for you.

1. Look back over your life. What are the main signs of God's presence and action?
2. Mary did not fully understand the actions of Jesus. What is your reaction when faced with something you do not understand?
3. Mary pondered everything in her heart. Ponder on the presence and action of God in your life. What response is being called forth from you?

Respond

Communicating with God goes beyond thinking, and sometimes we have to lay aside our own words and thoughts and give space to the heart for "the heart has its reasons of which the reason knows nothing" (Blaise Pascal). Let your heart respond to God's advances. There is no right or wrong response; there is only your response.

The prayer below might help in this process.

> *O Mary, immensity of heaven,*
> *foundation of the earth,*

depth of the seas, light of the sun,
beauty of the moon,
splendour of the stars in the heavens...
Your womb bore God,
before whose majesty man stands in awe.[47]

Rest

The story of Jesus staying behind in Jerusalem while his parents return home is not just an interesting little family vignette. Luke is revealing who Jesus is. Mary and Joseph have difficulty in grasping all the implications of this. Then Jesus is pictured as returning home with them, where he grows up like any young boy. Luke presents Mary as the model disciple as she thought deeply about all that was happening. Faith does not bring an absolute certainty; we have to struggle in order to integrate our faith with the events of daily life.

Just as Jesus took time to grow up, so also our prayer life will go through a process of maturation. The very popular Carmelite saint, Thérèse of Lisieux, was at the same time afraid and yet totally fearless. Her fear came from her knowledge of what it means to accept totally God's gift of love, and yet her lack of fear was due to her boundless confidence in God. Thérèse had great desires to do wonderful things for God. She wanted to convert the whole world; she wanted to be a missionary; she wanted to be a martyr, and so on. We know how she was tormented by unfulfilled longings, until she read chapters twelve and thirteen of the *First Letter to the Corinthians* in which she discovered her vocation to be love in the heart of the Church, her Mother.[48]

Thérèse had an intense desire to love and to do good, but at the same time she realised that she did not have the strength even to walk to the foothills of Mount Carmel, never mind ascend to the summit. She considered herself too small to do great things for God, but she did not give in to discouragement in the face of a seemingly impossible task. She realised that God had given her these great desires, and God would certainly fulfil them. So, in spite of her nothingness, she aspired to be what God wanted her to be – a saint.[49] Thérèse found the lift

---

47 Part of a Eucharistic Prayer of the Ethiopian Church, quoted in Sarah Jane Boss, *Mary*, New Century Theology Series, (London & New York: Continuum, 2004), pp. 8-9.

48 *Story of a Soul*, Manuscript B, 3v. Thérèse's autobiography, *Story of a Soul*, consists of three parts. Manuscript A is the first part of her life story, written at the request of her sister and prioress, Agnes of Jesus. Manuscript B is a letter addressed to her blood sister and sister in community, Marie of the Sacred Heart, and tells of Thérèse discovering her vocation to be love in the heart of the Church. Manuscript C is addressed to her prioress at the time, Marie de Gonzague, and speaks of her mature spiritual intuitions.

49 Ms. C, 2v.

that would carry her up to Jesus himself, and which would dispense her from climbing up the rough ladder of perfection. From reading certain Old Testament passages, she came to realise that the lift which would carry her to perfection was the arms of the Lord.[50] Thérèse wanted above all to love, but she found that she could not. However, she also discovered the solution to the impossibilities that her ambitions to love encountered. God puts the flame of love into the hearts of those who are willing to be consumed.

Thérèse's desire was to be a saint. She knew that she could never be like one of the great saints and so she was perfectly happy to be a 'little' saint. In her way of thinking, holiness consisted in consenting to whatever Jesus wanted to do in her, receiving his love when and how he chose to manifest it. She was content to appear before the Lord with empty hands because she believed that she would receive everything from God.

The popularity of Saint Thérèse can be explained by the fact that people intuitively see in her one who was totally open to God, and in whom God's merciful love triumphed. She was completely available to God no matter what the cost. This is the attitude of a contemplative. Thérèse never thought of herself as special; she was one of God's little ones. By seeking to do what Thérèse did, that is, do whatever we believe God is asking of us at each moment, we will be intimate friends of God, without necessarily being aware of it, and we will become what God knows we can be. This is the goal of the contemplative journey. Saint Thérèse points the way to all who wish to begin this journey, and her example encourages them to continue the journey when the night is darkest. Her purified faith allowed her to believe in the light, despite the darkness that surrounded her. Those who truly consent to the transforming presence and action of God in their lives will also be led safely through the valley of darkness to where God desires them to be. The contemplative way is the way of abandonment into the arms of a loving God.[51]

Take some time now to consent to God's transforming presence and action in your life. You do not need words; your silent desire will be understood by God.

---

50 Ms. C, 3r. Especially important for Thérèse's understanding were the Bible passages *Proverbs* 9:4 and *Isaiah* 66:12. On how Thérèse read the Scriptures, see Johan Bergström-Allen, T.O.C., & Wilfrid McGreal, O.Carm., (eds.), *The Gospel Sustains Me: The word of God in the life and love of Saint Thérèse of Lisieux,* (Faversham & Rome: Saint Albert's Press & Edizioni Carmelitane, 2009).
51 Cf. Ms. B, 1v.

Act

Mary pondered on everything that happened to her in order to discern the presence and action of God in the ordinary events of daily life. Try to live on a deeper level today as you go about your daily tasks. Where is God in all this busyness? Try to plug yourself in to the Source that connects the whole of creation. All that has life has come from, and is returning to, Life Itself. Human beings have been given the great gift of becoming aware of our Source and Goal. It is a tragedy to live an animal-like existence. Oscar Wilde was perhaps a little over dramatic when he said, "We are all in the gutter, but some of us are looking at the stars", yet he does have a point.

Try to be aware of your connection to all things and all people. Above all, seek to be aware of the presence and action of God in your life today.

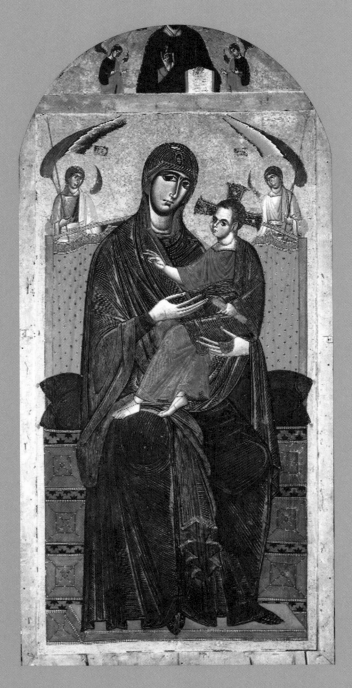

'La Madonna del Populo' (Our Lady of the People)
icon in the Brancacci Chapel of the Carmine (Carmelite Friary) in Florence, Italy.

THE BLESSEDNESS OF MARY

Luke 11:27-28

Opening Prayer

Loving God, you sent your Son as the Word that enlightens all people. Help me to listen to this Word and make it the lamp for my steps. Through Christ Our Lord. Amen.

Text

Read attentively the following Scripture text for the first time in order to get an idea of the overall sense and to take in the details. The version of the Bible from which we have taken our passage below is quite modern. It is part of a series of studies on the books of the New Testament, entitled *Sacra Pagina* (the Latin for 'Sacred Page', an ancient term for the Bible).[52] Each volume in the series provides a commentary on the Bible text as well as a new translation by one of a team of Catholic biblical scholars. If you want to really get into a particular part of the New Testament, it would be difficult to find better commentaries.

[27] As Jesus was saying these things, a woman shouted from the crowd, "Blessed is the womb that carried you and the breasts that fed you." [28] But he responded, "Blessed rather are those who hear the word of God and keep it."

Read

The shout of the unknown woman is an indirect compliment to Jesus, unique to Luke's Gospel. Jesus has just been fundamentally rejected by his opponents who claimed that he cast out demons by the power of the Prince of demons (*Luke* 11:15), so this blessing by the woman seems to be a positive response to that scurrilous claim. However, Jesus makes clear that the response he is seeking is not personal praise, but rather the hearing and keeping of God's word.

---

52   Luke T. Johnson, 'The Gospel of Luke', *Sacra Pagina*, Volume 3, edited by D. J. Harrington, (Collegeville, Minnesota: Liturgical Press, 1991), p. 34, © The Order of Saint Benedict, reprinted with permission.

The blessing on Jesus by proclaiming the blessedness of Jesus' mother echoes the benediction of Mary in *Luke* 1:42, 45, and 48. Jesus does not deny the blessing on his mother, but uses the opportunity presented to point to the basis of blessing for all disciples: those who hear God's Word and obey it will be blessed (cf. *Luke* 8:15, 21).

Reflect

Read again the text of *Luke* 11:27-28.

If we always think that the Word of God agrees with us, we are seriously fooling ourselves. The Word enlightens us, and therefore will correct our mistaken ideas or redirect our steps if we are going astray. However, we can refuse to allow the Word close enough to shine its light on our lives, because fundamentally we do not want to change. Reflection on the Word of God is intended to lead to an interiorisation of its message. The questions below are intended to assist in this process.

1. What does the Word of God mean to you?
2. How does the Word of God affect your daily life?
3. How does the Word of God enter into the way you make decisions?
4. Can you remember any time you felt challenged by the Word of God?

Respond

There is a time to reflect, and a time for the heart to communicate directly with God. What is in your heart? Do you want to complain to God, or perhaps to thank God for something? Whatever it is, it can be shared with God.

The unusual prayer below is intended to start you off. It is an adaptation of Saint Paul's hymn to Christ in the *Letter to the Philippians* (2:6-11) and applied to Our Lady.

> *Mary, though she was the Mother of God,*
> *did not count her closeness to God*
> *as something to hold on to,*
> *but emptied herself*
> *calling herself a servant,*
> *and living in the likeness of all other women.*
> *She humbled herself and stayed hidden,*
> *obedient to God, to the death of her Son,*
> *even death on a cross.*

Therefore God has highly exalted her
and bestowed on her the name,
which, after Jesus, is above every name,
that at the name of Mary
every head should bow,
in heaven and on earth and under the earth,
and every tongue confess
that Mary is the Mother of the Lord
to the glory of God the Father. Amen![53]

Rest

The 'false self' (as was discussed in reflection 8) will grasp on to anything to get what it wants. The false self is shorthand for our tendency to seek security for ourselves. Religion is intended to open us to God, but we can use it to bolster our own self-image. There was nothing wrong with what the woman in the crowd called out in our Scripture text, but Jesus took the opportunity to point out that, rather than claiming a physical relationship with him, it was far better to hear the word of God and keep it. Jesus said in another place that it is pointless to call him "Lord, Lord" and not do what he tells us (*Luke* 6:46).

What matters then is not the fact that we call ourselves Christians, but how we actually live day in and day out. Authentic prayer will have an effect on how we act and react. Usually the effects will not be dramatic, but it is more like the constant drip of water on rock; eventually the water will wear the rock away. Gradually our motives will be laid bare. Why do we pray? Some people 'meditate' in order to relax, or for other physical or psychological benefits. Prayer, on the other hand, is a relationship with God, and we cannot have a profound relationship if we seek to use the other person for our benefit. Perhaps we can fool people for a time, but we certainly cannot fool God. Very often, at the beginning of the relationship with God, we are attracted by what we get out of it, but these pleasant feelings sooner or later dry up. I have already mentioned (in reflection 9) the teaching of Saint John of the Cross on the 'dark night', or at least the first part of it. If we are serious about the relationship with God, our motivation will soon be challenged. The purpose of this is not to punish us in any way, but to help us grow up. God weans us off the spiritual milk to give us solid food, and for a while we will not be too happy. It is as if the light has gone

---

53 Raniero Cantalamessa, O.F.M.Cap., *Mary, Mirror of the Church*, (Collegeville, Minnesota: The Liturgical Press, 1992), p. 138.

out, and we cannot see the familiar objects around us. It takes a while for our eyes to adjust to the lack of light and for us to get used to the change of diet.

On the spiritual path our motivation will gradually be purified so that we will not be subtly seeking our own benefit instead of allowing God to accomplish his will in and through us. We should not be too quick to insist that our motivation is completely pure. I think that it is probably completely purified in the passage to eternal life. Until then, we have to struggle with our human nature, and the selfish element in every person to seek our own benefit even in the holiest pursuit. On the way of prayer, great honesty is required as we will be shown where our motivation is not quite pure. However, we have to exercise humility, which simply means to know and accept the truth about ourselves, in order to accept that we are not as holy as we secretly thought. We have to listen and be on the watch as God will reveal us to ourselves in different ways. It may come in a comment from someone. Our initial reaction might be to reject outright what has been said, but if we can look at the comment honestly at a later stage, perhaps there is an important message in it for us.

Spend some time now in the presence of God. Silently consent to God's purifying action within you.

Act

Mary led a hidden life for much of the time. She too had to listen to the Word of God, proclaimed by her Son, and act on it. How is God purifying your motives at the present stage of your life? Try and do something kind for someone else today without seeking any benefit at all, whether obvious or hidden, for yourself.

Mary in the Gospel of John

The Evangelist John depicted as an eagle.
Ceramic by Adam Kossowski in St. Joseph's Chapel, Aylesford Priory, Kent, England.

John's Gospel is clearly very different from the other three, although they do have many things in common. John tells fewer stories about what Jesus did, and his emphasis is always on what the different events reveal about Jesus. The reader is invited to discover the presence of God in Jesus. The whole of John's Gospel is based on the belief that Jesus is the Incarnate Word of God. Jesus provides unique and unprecedented access to God because he shares God's own nature. The Good News is the revelation of God in Jesus. What Jesus reveals about God comes through what he reveals about himself. After Jesus' death and return to God, his presence will continue in the Church by means of the Holy Spirit, or the Paraclete (to use John's terminology).

The author of John's Gospel is anonymous, like the other Gospels. Later tradition identifies them with some important figures in Christian history. John's Gospel depends for its authority on "the disciple whom Jesus loved". This figure, probably well-known to the community within which the Gospel was written, remains unknown to us. He is usually said to be John, one of the Twelve Apostles of Jesus, but it is impossible to be certain.

Before any part of the New Testament came to be written, stories circulated about what Jesus had said and what he had done. These were passed on by word of mouth, and perhaps some of them were written down, though the latter have not been discovered so far. In the first century communications were not as easy as they are today, and different stories or different forms of the same stories would have circulated in different communities. It seems that John's Gospel depends on an independent, though similar, source or sources to that or those used for the writing of the other Gospels.

The likely date of the Fourth Gospel is between 80-100 A.D. The social situation to which it refers is the struggle within Judaism after the destruction of Jerusalem by the Roman armies that took place in 70 A.D. This event was cataclysmic for Jews and it set off, or intensified, an internal struggle wherever Jews lived in the Roman Empire. The struggle was over what Judaism was, how it was to be developed, and who was a Jew. The party of the Pharisees won the struggle, and this goes some way to explain the bad press they receive in the Gospels. It was decided that Christians were heretics and were to be expelled from the synagogues. This was a crisis for the people who believed that Jesus was the Messiah. It also is the key to understand the vehement language sometimes used against "the Jews" in John's Gospel. This term is not against all Jewish people, although it has often been used this way to tragic results; "the Jews" in John's Gospel usually refers to the religious leaders who had been responsible for handing Jesus over to be crucified, and who had been responsible for expelling Christian Jews from the synagogue.

The Gospel is shaped by images from the Old Testament. The very first words, "In the beginning..." were intended to evoke the beginning of creation in the book of *Genesis*. The author of the Gospel clearly knows very well and loves the Scriptures. The Gospel of John was written by a Jewish-Christian for and in a

Jewish-Christian community that was in conflict with the synagogue authorities of its day (represented in the Gospel as "the Pharisees" or "the Jews").

Mary is present in two events recounted by John: at the marriage feast of Cana (2:1-11) and at the crucifixion of Jesus (19:25-27). In *John* 6:42, where the people say that they know the mother and father of Jesus, there is a reference to Mary, but she herself does not appear in the scene. However, this is an important reference because it shows the opinion of the local people, but does it also express the opinion of the Evangelist?

Like Mark, John tells us nothing about Jesus' birth, although he does refer to his pre-existence. He shows us Mary with her already grownup son. In his Gospel, three distinctive elements are to be noted. First, the two scenes where Jesus and Mary appear together are at the beginning and end of his public activity. Secondly, the Gospel stresses that she is the mother of Jesus. John's Gospel uses this term "the mother of Jesus" six times, almost as a title, and she is never given her proper name. The Fourth Evangelist is primarily interested in Mary's relation to Jesus. Thirdly on both occasions, the disciples of Jesus are involved.[54]

---

54   See Klemens Stock, S.J., *Mary the Mother of the Lord in the New Testament*, (Rome: Edizioni Carmelitane, 2006), p. 111.

The icon of Our Lady of Hope, written by the Carmelite nuns in Ravenna, Italy, as a focus of prayer during the 'Pilgrimage of Hope' to Rome of young people associated with the Carmelite Order in Europe, July 2010.

THE MOTHER OF JESUS AT CANA
John 2:1-12

Opening Prayer

Gracious God, you call all people to the banquet of eternal life where we will celebrate the triumph of your love. Help me to listen to your Word and be refreshed with the abundance of your new wine. I make this prayer through Christ, Our Lord. Amen.

Text

Read attentively the following Scripture text for the first time in order to get an idea of the overall sense and to take in the details. The Bible translation used for the passage is derived from the Latin version (the 'Vulgate') of Saint Jerome (345-420). The English translation of the Vulgate was made in the late-16th and early-17th centuries by Roman Catholics who had escaped from the persecution of their faith in England, as is known as the *Douay-Rheims Bible* from the place where they lived on the Continent.[55] The translation was substantially revised by Bishop Challoner in the middle of the 18th century.

1 And the third day, there was a marriage in Cana of Galilee: and the mother of Jesus was there. 2 And Jesus also was invited, and his disciples, to the marriage. 3 And the wine failing, the mother of Jesus saith to him: They have no wine. 4 And Jesus saith to her: Woman, what is that to me and to thee? My hour is not yet come. 5 His mother saith to the waiters: Whatsoever he shall say to you, do ye. 6 Now there were set there six waterpots of stone, according to the manner of the purifying of the Jews, containing two or three measures apiece. 7 Jesus saith to them: Fill the waterpots with water. And they filled them up to the brim. 8 And Jesus saith to them: Draw out now and carry to the chief steward of the feast. And they carried it. 9 And when the chief steward had tasted the water made wine and knew not whence it was, but the waiters knew who had drawn the water: the chief steward calleth the bridegroom, 10

---

55 *The Holy Bible: Douay-Rheims Version*, edited by J. Gibbons and translated by Bishop R. Challoner, available in various editions.

And saith to him: Every man at first setteth forth good wine, and when men have well drunk, then that which is worse. But thou hast kept the good wine until now. [11] This beginning of miracles did Jesus in Cana of Galilee and manifested his glory. And his disciples believed in him. [12] After this, he went down to Capharnaum, he and his mother and his brethren and his disciples: and they remained there not many days.

Read

The Gospel of John presents us principally with an understanding of who is Jesus Christ. This is true also for the story of the marriage feast at Cana. However, what the Evangelist has to say about Mary, the mother of Jesus, is not unimportant. What interests John is the relationship she has with her son. The mystery of Mary is only understood in relationship with the mystery of Christ.

The situation of the story is that of a wedding feast, but John seems to have little interest in the happy couple, their parents, etc. Instead, the focus of this story is on Jesus, his mother and his disciples. There are many indications in the text that we are not dealing with a simple story about a wedding and an action by Jesus to relieve the embarrassment of the couple over the wine running out. The Gospel writer is telling us something important by means of a story. Over the centuries there have been innumerable interpretations of this story. I will suggest only one, but one which I believe has a lot of truth in it.[56] This story is the culmination of the various events in the first chapter of John's Gospel, where Jesus has been revealing himself to his disciples. Jesus is forming a new community and eliciting faith from his disciples. This self-revelation and forming of a community of faith is a constant theme in the whole Gospel.

Jesus' mother asks nothing explicit of him in verse 3. She simply makes known the situation of the lack of wine, but his response in verse 4 makes clear that her words carried an implied request. Jesus' mother assumed her son would somehow attend to the problem. Jesus' words to his mother sound harsh to the modern ear, but they are neither rude nor hostile. Jesus lets his mother know that while she might be concerned with a material problem, he is focused on a spiritual reality. It seems that Jesus certainly places a distance between the former relationship he had with his mother and points towards the new

56 See Ignace de la Potterie, *Mary in the Mystery of the Covenant*, (New York: Alba House, Society of St. Paul, 1992), pp. 157-208.

relationship between Jesus as the Messiah and Mary as representing the whole of Israel.

Mary does not understand Jesus' response as a refusal. She tells the servants, "Do whatever he tells you", or in the rather old Bible translation used for this text, "Whatsoever he shall say to you, do ye". This is not a simple request on the material level, but has profound spiritual implications. Mary goes to Jesus and she leads others to him. They must look to him and receive their instructions from him. It is interesting to note that the word which is translated in our text as "waiters" is used by John elsewhere to signify the true disciples of Jesus (cf. *John* 12:26).

The jars from which the new wine is drawn (verse 8) were filled to the brim (verse 7). Since each jar had a large capacity – about 20 to 30 gallons – Jesus turned an astonishing quantity of water into wine. The extravagance is at the heart of the miracle because it refers to the superabundance of gifts available through Jesus. He is the real Groom who has kept "the good wine until now" (verse 10).

Our text in verse 11 says that this was the "beginning of miracles". The word that John actually uses might more appropriately be translated as "sign" or "symbol". The fact that Jesus has kept the good wine until now, and the fact that it is so abundant, are symbols of the new life that he is offering to all who believe in him.

What we have here is not the simple story of a wedding where Jesus performs a miracle. It is a profound reflection on the person of Jesus as Messiah. He offers us the good wine, and Mary, as his intimate collaborator, continually encourages us to do whatever he tells us.

Reflect

Read again the text of *John* 2:1-12.

In order to help you apply this text to your own life, I have suggested some questions. If they are a help, please use them. If not, perhaps you have your own way to allow the Word of God to penetrate the reality of your life.

1. Who is Jesus Christ for you?
2. What needs in your own life, and in the lives of others, do you want to present to him?
3. How do you take no response from him to your requests?

4. Are you prepared to do whatever he tells you?
5. What do you think the "best wine" might be for you?

Respond

This is the time to let your heart speak directly to God. Perhaps the prayer below will help, but what is important is that you communicate directly with God, expressing what is in your heart.

> *With loving care for the bridegroom and his bride*
> *she turns to her Son for help*
> *and tells the servants to do what he commands.*
> *Water is changed into wine,*
> *the wedding guests rejoice,*
> *as Christ foreshadows the wedding feast*
> *that is his daily gift to his Bride, the Church.*
>
> *In this great sign*
> *the presence of the Messiah is proclaimed,*
> *the outpouring of the Holy Spirit is foretold,*
> *and the hour of salvation is foreshadowed*
> *when Christ will clothe himself*
> *with the royal robes of his passion*
> *to shed his blood on the cross*
> *for his Bride, the Church.*
>
> *Through him the angels of heaven*
> *offer their prayer of adoration*
> *as they rejoice in your presence for ever.*
> *May our voices be one with theirs*
> *in their triumphant hymn of praise.*[57]

Rest

Mary, the Mother of Jesus, knows our situation – "they have no wine" (2:3) – and presents this constantly to her Son. She points to him and tells us to do whatever he tells us (cf. 2:5). Pope Saint Gregory the Great pointed out, "The fundamental preparation for contemplation, of course, is the devout living of the Christian life through the power of the Holy Spirit expressed in the virtues

---

57 From the Eucharistic Preface 'Our Lady of Cana', in *Masses of the Blessed Virgin Mary* (New York: Catholic Book Publishing Co., 1992), p. 114.

of faith, hope and charity, and the increasing activity of the sevenfold gift".[58] Therefore, doing what the Lord tells us is vital in the Christian life. "It is not those who say, "Lord, Lord" who will enter the kingdom of heaven, but the one who does the will of my father in heaven" (*Matthew* 7:21). The supreme value of Christianity is not contemplation but love. Contemplation is not an end in itself; it is a means to arrive at union with God. Contemplation is not the reward for great virtue or much time spent in prayer, but is that which makes us capable of great virtue, of great love. However, the readiness to encounter God immediately and directly in contemplation normally presupposes perseverance at some form of personal prayer for a considerable length of time.

God will transform us through the intimate communication we call prayer, but this involves our co-operation. The Christian life is not a solitary struggle to keep the commandments, nor does it work by magic absolving us from all effort. According to Saint Paul, Christ has already opened the way for all of us to enter God's family. There are no more exclusions, but our co-operation is required (cf. *Romans* 8 in particular). Contemplation and mysticism were frowned upon for many years, partly because of the split between faith and life. Some who claimed to be great contemplatives in fact did not even live a basic moral life. If we are praying in the sense of being open to God, we will be constantly challenged in many ways to address situations in our lives that need attention. It is, of course, possible for the 'false self' (as discussed in reflection 8) to use even prayer for its own purposes.

Fundamentally the false self is seeking security for itself in any way it can get it. If you choose to take your spiritual life seriously, this does not affect the false self, which simply changes its focus. Instead of seeking security in material things, it begins to seek security in spiritual things. If people think I am very holy because I have a pious look about me, I can always claim that I am certainly doing nothing to influence them, but secretly I might begin to believe my own publicity.

Searing honesty and a willingness to work directly against the false self are essential for the spiritual journey. The first fruit of authentic prayer is self-knowledge, which always remains an essential part of a healthy spiritual life.[59] We cannot come to know God without learning a great deal about ourselves and

---

58 Quoted in Bernard McGinn, *The Growth of Mysticism: The Presence of God*, A History of Western Christian Mysticism Series, (London: SCM Press, 1994), p. 56.

59 This was realised by the great Carmelite saint Teresa of Jesus (of Avila), in her *Interior Castle*, I,2,8-9. There are two important English translations of Teresa's writings. The earlier is the edition by E. Allison Peers, *Complete Works of St. Teresa*, (London: Sheed & Ward, 1957). The later is edited by Kieran Kavanaugh, O.C.D., & Otilio Rodriguez, O.C.D., *The Collected Works of St. Teresa of Avila*, (Washington D.C.: I.C.S. Publications, 1976-85), 3 volumes.

often this is very painful. When we learn some painful facts about ourselves, we must try to do something about them. Our prayer will not go well if we refuse to give up some sin or some manifestation of the false self. "No matter how high your contemplation may be, seek always to begin and end your prayer with the knowledge of yourselves," advised John of the Cross.[60]

Take some time now to be yourself before God. In silence let God speak to your heart. Try not to put up any barriers to this communication. Let go of your own words, ideas and thoughts, and just be in God's presence.

Act

The story of the marriage feast at Cana features a miracle of Jesus to give joy to people, although the joy is much more than just an extra glass of wine; it is the offer of eternal life. Mary is also pictured as presenting the need to Jesus, and encouraging people to do whatever he tells them. Perhaps you could do something kind for another person today or at least present their needs to the Lord in prayer.

---

60 *Spiritual Canticle*, 39.5.

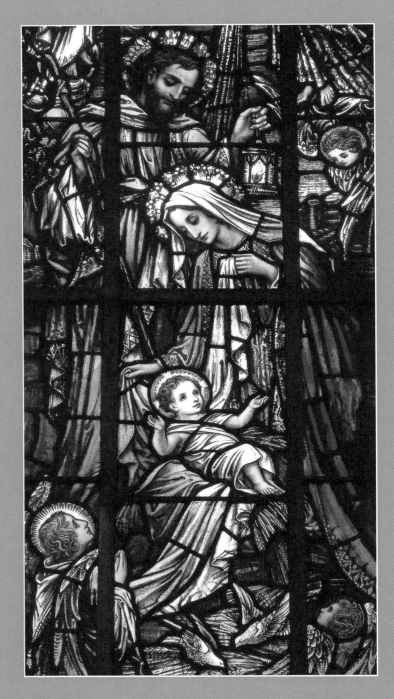

The infant Jesus with Mary and Joseph.
Window at Whitefriar Street Carmelite Church, Dublin, Ireland.

WE KNOW HIS FATHER AND MOTHER
John 6:42; cf. 1:45; Matthew 13:55; Luke 4:22

Opening Prayer

O God, I give you thanks for life and for all the gifts you have so generously bestowed. Help me to accept others as they are, your beloved children, and not judge them from my own narrow perspective. Help me to listen to your Word, that it might open me to your truth. Amen.

Text

Read attentively the following verse of Scripture for the first time in order to get an idea of the overall sense and to take in the details. The *Christian Community Bible* translation comes from the Philippines and was made in 1988. The translation was specifically intended for basic Christian communities to study the Bible together.[61]

> [42] And they said, "This man is the son of Joseph, isn't he? We know his father and mother. How can he say that he has come from heaven?"

Read

We can compare this verse with *John* 1:45-51 where Jesus is referred to as the "son of Joseph", as well as with *Luke* 4:22. Taken literally, this obviously affects belief in the virgin birth that is clearly held by the writers of the Gospels of Matthew and Luke (see also reflection five in this book on *Mark* 6:1-6).

The text of *John* 6:42 forms part of the famous speech by Jesus in which he reveals himself as the bread of life. He had just performed a miracle by feeding a multitude (*John* 6:1-13, and the same story in the other Gospels: *Matthew* 14:15-21; 15:32-39; *Mark* 6:30-44; 8:1-10; *Luke* 9:12-17). In John's Gospel the people respond by trying to proclaim Jesus king. Jesus then tries to bring the people to a more spiritual understanding of who he is. He tells them that he

---

61   *Christian Community Bible: Catholic Pastoral Edition*, Second Edition, 1988 © Pastoral Bible Foundation, (printed in various editions by Claretian Publications / St. Paul Publications / Divine Word Publications).

is the bread of life, and that whoever comes to him will never be hungry. He does not seem to have much success, because the people cannot understand what on earth he is talking about. Then comes the text we are considering now, where the people express their amazement at what Jesus is saying. They claim to know where he comes from, and who his mother and father are. Therefore it is impossible for him to "come from heaven".

This text – and the earlier one in *John* 1:45 where Philip, the future apostle, calls Jesus "the son of Joseph" – have been used by some experts on the Bible to try to show that the Fourth Evangelist had no knowledge of the virgin birth, or that he did not believe it. However, it seems clear when one tries to read the Scriptures without undue bias, that this term is used to express the common opinion of the people about Jesus before coming to faith in him. Therefore, it certainly would not be the opinion of the Gospel writer. In the speech about the bread of life, Jesus goes on to speak about his Father, who is God. John's Gospel can be very subtle, and it must be read attentively if it is to be understood the way that John wants his readers to understand. He uses the common opinion of the people – that Jesus is the son of Joseph from Nazareth – to present his own Christian faith, that in fact Jesus is the Son of God and has come down from heaven in order to bring life to all.

Reflect

Read again the text of *John* 6:42.

There are many opinions about Jesus Christ in our days, and indeed he has always attracted controversy, as was prophesied by Simeon, when he was presented in the Temple by Mary and Joseph (*Luke* 2:34). Our view of Christ will affect how we understand the place of Mary, his Mother, and vice versa. In the short text that we have been considering, John contrasts the common opinion of the people, based on their knowledge of Jesus' background, to the revelation that he is the Son of God.

What does it mean for you that Jesus is the Son of God? The questions below are intended to help you reflect on this central doctrine of the Christian faith, and particularly how it relates to your own life.

1. What is your relationship with Jesus Christ and his Mother?
2. How do you feed these relationships?
3. When does an opinion about Jesus Christ become faith in him?

4. How does Mary point you towards her Son?
5. What does it mean for you that Jesus is the Son of God?

Respond

It is time to give your heart free rein. The purpose of prayer is to open you to the purifying and transforming presence of God. What springs up from your heart now? The prayer below might help you to be as you are before God, without any mask or pretence.

> I greet you, rose garden of heaven,
> the chosen, the pure, the tender one.
> You noble sweet rose blossom,
> entreat God for me through your goodness. [62]

Rest

John of the Cross wrote "What we need most in order to make progress is to be silent before this great God with our appetites and our tongue, for the language He best hears is silent love". [63] The mere absence of thoughts, emotions, activity or distractions does not constitute prayer of any kind. As Thomas Merton wrote, "An emptiness that is deliberately cultivated, for the sake of fulfilling a personal spiritual ambition, is not empty at all: it is full of itself. It is so full that the light of God cannot get into it anywhere." [64] However, progress in prayer is often characterised by the gradual transformation of many words and thoughts into the simplicity of loving surrender.

We need to learn how to become silent. It is rather like gazing into someone's eyes. This is actually a very intimate thing to do, and therefore cannot be done with many people. If you try this with someone you hardly know, it is liable to give offence. You will have to spend some considerable time becoming close to the other person before trying to gaze into his or her eyes. When eventually you are close enough to the other to do the gazing bit, you move beyond the need for many words. There is a time for words and a time for silence, and you must know the difference. In a human relationship it takes a little while to become sensitive to the needs of the other person in order to pick up when it is good to speak, and when it is better to communicate in another way. The trouble with words is that they can actually be used to avoid communication. Jesus said that

---

62 From a 14th-century German prayer, quoted in John D. Miller, *Beads and Prayers: The Rosary in History and Devotion*, (London & New York: Burns & Oates & Continuum, 2002), p. 49.
63 *Maxims*, 53.
64 Thomas Merton, O.C.S.O., *Contemplative Prayer*, (New York: Image Books/Doubleday, 1990), p. 94.

we should not babble as the pagans do, thinking that we would be heard by God because of our many words (*Matthew* 6:7).

With silence we can communicate many emotions. Can you communicate your love and desire for God in silence? Perhaps you will find a prayer word useful to maintain your gaze fixed on God. See the section "Rest" in reflection 10 for further information on methods that use a prayer word.

Act

Prayer divorced from life lacks an essential component. Both have to affect each other. If your life is in turmoil, it is not realistic to expect that your prayer will be sweetness and light. If you are seeking to escape problems in your life by fleeing to an imaginary world where all is well, you are not seeking God but yourself. God may comfort you in the midst of trials but perhaps God is telling you something important by means of these difficulties. If you do not listen to the voice of God in daily life, you will not hear this still, small voice at the time of prayer.

Your prayer is a time to fine tune your spiritual sensitivity so that you will be able to receive God's communications throughout the day. Jesus was much more than the people imagined him to be. Be open today to the possibility that the people you meet and the things you experience may be more than you imagine them to be. Perhaps they are the vehicles of God's communication to you. Be alert for the approach of God under the disguise of ordinary people and ordinary events.

Mary with the crucified Christ (Pietà),
at CISA (Saint Albert's International Centre), Rome, Italy.

MARY AT THE FOOT OF THE CROSS
John 19:25b-27

Opening Prayer

O God, your Son breathed out the Spirit as he died on the cross. Send forth your Spirit upon me as I contemplate your Word. Help me to be a faithful member of the family he constituted, and so become his beloved disciple. Through Christ Our Lord. Amen.

Text

Read attentively the following Bible text for the first time in order to get an idea of the overall sense and to take in the details. The translation below, *The Webster Bible*, comes from the work of Noah Webster, an American scholar of the 19th century.[65] He revised the *King James Authorised Version* of the Bible to make it more usable in schools of his day. In fact he changed as little as possible.

> 25b Now there stood by the cross of Jesus, his mother, and his mother's sister, Mary [the wife] of Cleophas, and Mary Magdalene. 26 When Jesus therefore saw his mother, and the disciple standing by, whom he loved, he saith to his mother, Woman, behold thy son! 27 Then saith he to the disciple, Behold thy mother! And from that hour that disciple took her to his own [home].

Read

The Bible translation for this reading is rather old but hopefully is still understandable. The words in the square brackets – "wife" and "home" – are not in the original Greek text but have been put in by the translator to make the meaning more understandable. Indeed most English translations of the Bible have these words.

John's Gospel has been leading up to the moment of Jesus' crucifixion. Now his "hour" has arrived, and this is the culmination of the revelation of who Jesus

---

65 Noah Webster, (ed.), *The Holy Bible, Containing the Old and New Testaments, in the Common Version, with Amendments of the Language*, (New Haven: Durrie and Peck, 1833, reprinted Grand Rapids: Baker Book House, 1987).

is. The crucifixion is narrated in five scenes, the centre of which is Jesus' words to his mother.

The list of women in *John* 19:25b is different from the lists in *Mark* 15:40 and *Matthew* 27:56. The only name they share in common is Mary Magdalene. In Matthew and Mark, the women are mentioned after the death of Jesus and they are said to be standing far off. Saint Luke's Gospel does not name the women. There have been all sorts of theories about who exactly these women are. A first question is: how many women were there? There could be three, if the sister of the mother of Jesus is also called Mary and is married to Cleophas, or there could be four if Our Lady's sister is unnamed. It seems preferable to say that there were four women, because then they are contrasted with the four soldiers in verses 23 and 24. These two scenes at the foot of the cross are very much connected. The soldiers do not divide Jesus' tunic, and this has often been taken to represent the unity of the People of God gathered together by Christ. The mother of Jesus and the disciple he loved are understood to symbolically represent the whole People.

There have been great debates about this scene at the foot of the cross, and they tend to divide along Catholic and Protestant lines. Catholics talk-up the role of Mary, the Mother of Jesus, and Protestants tend to talk-up the role of the disciple whom Jesus loved. They are obviously both important. This could be simply a sad scene where the dying Jesus asks his favourite disciple to take care of his mother. However, this is most unlikely, as John's Gospel tells stories for a good reason. He does not tell us anything about the birth or childhood of Jesus, so why would he bother about a simple, though moving, scene of an intimate family issue? Another question that arises is where are the "brothers and sisters of Jesus"? Why would Jesus entrust his mother into the care of a disciple if Mary had other children?

It is clear that John is telling us something important by means of this scene. Jesus addresses his mother as "woman". Our attention is drawn to the only other scene in John's Gospel where the mother of Jesus is present – the marriage feast at Cana (2:1-12). There too, Jesus calls his mother "woman". There certainly is intended to be a connection. The two scenes in John's Gospel are at the beginning and end of Jesus' public ministry. Through the instigation of his mother, Jesus understands at Cana that the Father is asking him to begin his public ministry, and here at the foot of the cross he binds together his mother and the disciple whom he loved. At Cana, Jesus told his mother that his hour had not yet come. At the foot of the cross, when his "hour" had finally arrived, he poured out in abundance the good wine that had been preserved until that moment.

In the scene at the foot of the cross, there are three people who are not named. John goes to the trouble of telling us that Mary of Cleophas (normally meaning that she was married to him) and Mary Magdalene were present. Why then does he not name the other three people in the scene? They obviously have important roles to play, as Jesus addresses them just before he dies. The mother of Jesus, her sister, and the disciple whom Jesus loved, are described rather than named. The most important thing about his mother and the disciple is not their name but their relationship to Jesus. You will note that the end of the text has, "And from that hour that disciple took her to his own [home]." A literal translation would be, "took her (or welcomed her) into his own". Most people assume that it is referring to his home, but could it also refer to something else? Could "his own" mean what is most precious to him, that is, his relationship to Jesus?[66] If that were the case, the disciple whom Jesus loved would be putting Mary in the midst of his relationship to Jesus. Mary is told that the disciple whom Jesus loved is to be her son. She has to take Jesus' disciples into her heart, and she has a very important role to play in their spiritual lives. The sister of Jesus' mother is not named, presuming she is not Mary of Cleophas. Could it be that it is her relationship to Mary that is being stressed?

In the verse following this scene, it says that Jesus knew that all was now accomplished. The symbolic significance of the undivided tunic was realised in Mary and the disciple. They represent the people whom God is calling around Jesus the Messiah. This is the birth of the Church, according to John, and so Jesus can, in truth, say that all is accomplished.

Reflect

Read again the text of *John* 19:25b-27. This Gospel scene is full of mystery. Why did John include it at this point? What does it say about Mary's relationship to each one of us? Reflection is not just an intellectual exercise but is intended to help us chew over the various elements of a passage, so that we can receive what God wants to say to us by means of it. Sometimes familiarity stops us from seeing something new; we think we know what the passage is about and we can miss God's message to us today. Below I have suggested some questions to assist you to reflect on the significance of this passage for your own life.

---

66 See Klemens Stock, S.J., *Mary the Mother of the Lord in the New Testament*, (Rome: Edizioni Carmelitane, 2006), p. 163.

1. What is the significance of those people who are named at the foot of the cross?
2. Some say that the disciple whom Jesus loved represents all of his disciples of all time. What does it mean for you to be a disciple loved by Jesus?
3. The Mother of Jesus is to be the mother of the beloved disciple. What part in your life does Mary have?

Respond

This is the time for your own heart to speak to the heart of God. Perhaps the words below will help to get you started. What is important, though, is that you communicate with God what is in your heart.

> O Lord, we praise and magnify your Name
> For the Most Holy Virgin-Mother of God,
> Who is the highest of your saints,
> The most glorious of all your creatures,
> The most perfect of all your works,
> The nearest to you, in the throne of God,
> Whom you were pleased to make
> Daughter of the Eternal Father,
> Mother of the Eternal Son,
> Spouse of the Eternal Spirit,
> Tabernacle of the most glorious Trinity.
> Mother of Jesus,
> Mother of the Messiah,
> Mother of the Desire of Nations,
> Mother of the Prince of Peace,
> Mother of the King of Heaven,
> Mother of our Creator,
> Mother and Virgin,
> Mirror of humility and obedience,
> Mirror of wisdom and devotion,
> Mirror of modesty and chastity,
> Mirror of sweetness and resignation.
> Mirror of sanctity,
> Mirror of all virtues.[67]

67 Thomas Traherne (1637-74), quoted in John Macquarrie, *Mary For All Christians*, (Edinburgh: T. & T. Clark, 1990, Second Edition 2001), p. 157.

Rest

We have already looked (in reflection 9) at the concept of the 'dark night' according to Saint John of the Cross. Actually, we looked only at the first part, often called 'the night of sense', which often occurs early on the spiritual journey. It is generally experienced as dryness when one tries to pray, and a lack of sensory pleasure in one's religious practices that formerly gave great satisfaction. The reason for this is to wean the individual away from these spiritual pleasures, in order that he or she will seek the God of all consolations and not all the consolations of God. Another way of understanding what is going on is that God is helping us to see that the 'false self' (discussed in reflection 8) has no future. The false self is not something outside of us; it is what we believe ourselves to be, and so we will not give it up without an almighty fight because we cannot imagine any other kind of self. Jesus said very clearly, and in different ways, that the one who seeks to save his life will lose it, and the one who loses his life for Christ's sake will save it (*Matthew* 10:39; cf. 16:24-25; *Luke* 9:23-24; 14:26-27; 17:33; *Mark* 8:34-35; *John* 12:25). The sayings of Jesus are often open to many interpretations, depending on the willingness of the individual to hear the message. No doubt Jesus was reminding his disciples of the radical nature of following him. It could have literally meant losing their lives. This has been the outcome many times for those who bear witness to Christ. However, his warning can also refer to the struggle that takes place on the spiritual journey when we attack the false self. It is fundamentally an illusion – how we present ourselves, how we want other people to see us and think of us. However, this illusion is so strong that we often believe there is nothing else. The 'true self' is who I am in God. It is who I am created to be, independent of how clever I am or of what I look like and how I speak. The true self is the core of my being which emerges from God at every moment. If I cling on to the false self and refuse to let go, it will be torn from me at death because how I present myself to the world dies. If, on the other hand, I have refused to be captivated by the siren calls of the false self and instead sought my true self in God, at death when the false self dies, what is left?

Death is a letting go of everything we have known and loved. If we have invested all our energies into this world, when the time comes to depart we will have nothing left. However, life itself is continually preparing us to let go by a thousand little deaths that range from the trivial to the devastating. These could be getting too fat to wear your favourite jeans, your football team losing the cup final, your dog dying, or the death of someone you love. Mary was warned that a sword would pierce her soul (*Luke* 2:35). She would share in the rejection experienced by her Son. In the Bible text we have been considering in this reflection, Mary stands at the foot of the cross watching her Son being executed as a criminal and rejected by the religious leaders of her people. Our Lady died a thousand deaths in preparation for her final journey to God.

The first stage of the dark night frees us from over-dependence on our senses in the relationship with God, who is outside our realm of experience. With our reason, we could grope towards the idea that there is a God, but we cannot have a relationship with an idea. It is only when God takes the initiative to approach us that we can move from 'knowing about' to 'knowing'. However, most of us carry a lot of baggage with us that we have picked up along the way. The first part of the dark night deals with the easy stuff, though it may not feel easy at the time. This does not happen all at once; it more likely comes and goes as we need to let go of something else in order to continue the journey into God. We might even have the experience of facing issues that we thought had been dealt with at an earlier period, but they return at a deeper level.

For some there comes another part of the 'night', usually when the individual has responded positively to the privations of the first part and remains faithful to God in prayer and in daily life. The transforming love of God changes the person's way of being in the world. Objectively such a person can lead a very moral life, committed to the spiritual path, but he or she becomes aware of the disorder that exists deep within. What was always there now becomes apparent to the individual: the roots of the false self that spoils even the best actions with self-seeking motives. The person becomes aware as never before of the gulf that exists between him or her and God. Of course the person always knew that God was far greater, yet normally felt a certain closeness, but in the 'night of spirit' the individual can feel that God has finally given up in disgust. This is, in fact, caused by the inflow of God into the soul that is too much for the person to bear, and it is experienced as darkness.[68]

John of the Cross maintains that the cause of this confusion and deep distress is, paradoxically, the light of God's love that is flooding into the person, because many of the blocks have been dissolved. In this light, we can see ourselves as we really are for the first time. We become aware of the holiness of God, and our own sinfulness, in a way that surpasses any earlier experience. In the Old Testament there was a profound belief that no one could see God and live (*Exodus* 33:20). In the New Testament we have several stories of the demons recognising who Jesus is and responding with fear (cf. *Luke* 4:41). Then we

---

68 John of the Cross, *The Dark Night*, I, 1-13.

have Simon Peter's interesting response to the huge catch of fish. Jesus told Peter to go out into the deep and put out his nets, but Peter objects that they have been toiling all night to no avail. Nevertheless, because Jesus has asked, he obeys. The result is astonishing, but when Peter sees it he is struck with terror, "Depart from me for I am a sinful man" (*Luke* 5:8). In the presence of Christ, Peter can see himself as he is.

Spend some time now in silence. Let God probe your heart. Mary stood at the foot of the cross and let go of her Son into the Father's arms. Ask her help to let go of your own ways of judging yourself and others. Consent to the presence and purifying action of God in your life.

Act

Is there anything you know in your heart of hearts of which you need to let go? Perhaps it is a way of acting, or a relationship. If we hold onto something and seek from it a type of happiness that it is not by nature capable of giving, we are treating it as an idol and putting it in the place of God. If we hold on to an idol, it will become a major block on our spiritual path.

Listen to the still small voice of God today as you go about your daily tasks. What is God asking of you?

Mary in the Other New Testament Writings

The Churches of Christ.
Ceramic by Adam Kossowski in St. Joseph's Chapel, Aylesford Priory, Kent, England.

Acts of the Apostles

There is no real agreement as to when the Gospel of Luke and the *Acts of the Apostles* were written, but probably around 80-85 A.D. *Acts* is the continuation of the story of Jesus in the lives of his followers. The activity of God's Spirit is paramount in *Acts* as the Christian message spreads from Jerusalem to Rome, the capital of the known-world.

Luke paints a vivid and varied image of Mary at the beginning of his Gospel. He also has Mary at the beginning of his second volume, where he describes the birth of the Church, the community of believers in Jesus the Christ.

The New Testament Letters

The New Testament includes 21 letters, placed between the *Acts of the Apostles* and the book of *Revelation* (also known as the *Apocalypse*). There are 13 letters which are normally attributed to Saint Paul. Some of these certainly have Saint Paul as their author, while others are disputed. These letters date from around 50-60 A.D., which makes them the earliest of the New Testament writings. Not included in the aforementioned 13 is the letter to the *Hebrews*; it was long thought to have Saint Paul as author, but almost certainly this is not the case.[69]

In all of the 21 letters, the mother of Jesus is mentioned only once. The occurrence is in Saint Paul's *Letter to the Galatians*, which we will consider below. Why is there so little interest in Mary? Paul focuses mostly on the meaning of Christ's death and resurrection, and our response. He spent a great deal of time struggling to make clear what the content of the first preaching about Jesus Christ should be, against those who wanted to make the message something different. Strangely, he shows little interest in the life of Jesus before his passion, and he rarely cites anything Jesus is reported to have said or done. We should perhaps then not be surprised about his seeming lack of interest in the mother of Jesus. It is only later generations of Christians that wanted to find out about the origins of Jesus.

The Book of Revelation

This book is often known as the *Apocalypse* and is perhaps the most difficult for modern readers to understand, as it uses a type of literature that seems very unusual to us. The author was heavily influenced by similar texts in the Old Testament. It was initially written to be heard in order to give hope in the midst of persecution. Very early tradition claimed that Saint John, the beloved disciple, wrote both the Fourth Gospel and the *Book of Revelation*. However, this has been seriously doubted for a very long time.

The author, whoever he was, probably was Palestinian by birth, and he wrote this work around 90-95 A.D., but an earlier date is possible. A long tradition has linked John's Gospel with *Revelation*. They are very different, but there are also some similarities of themes. There are also connections with the other Gospels. The author uses a complex interweaving of symbols from various ancient sources, but in particular the Old Testament.

---

69 For a Carmelite reflection on *Hebrews* see John FitzGerald, O.Carm., *Backwards into the Future: Meditations on the Letter to the Hebrews*, (Faversham: Saint Albert's Press, 2005).

Mary and the Apostles at prayer during Pentecost.
Painting by Adam Kossowski at the
Church of Our Lady of Mount Carmel, Faversham, Kent, England.

MARY IN THE PRIMITIVE CHURCH
Acts 1:13-14

Opening Prayer

Loving God, the disciples of your Son throughout the centuries have gathered in prayer together with Mary, his Mother. Help me to be aware of her presence with me, as I seek to be open to your Word. Through Christ Our Lord. Amen.

Text

Read attentively the following Bible text for the first time in order to get an idea of the overall sense and to take in the details. The translation of Scripture we are using in this reflection is a fruit of *The Anchor Bible Project* that began to produce volumes in 1956. Very many eminent scholars were involved in the project. The author of the translation of and commentary on *The Acts of the Apostles* is one of the foremost biblical scholars of his generation.[70]

[13] Entering the city, they went to the upper room where they were staying, Peter, John and James, Andrew, Philip and Thomas, Bartholomew, Matthew and James, son of Alphaeus, Simon the Zealot, and Judas, son of James. [14] They were all devoting themselves with one accord to prayer, together with some women and Mary, the mother of Jesus, as well as his brothers.

Read

For Luke, prayer as communing with God is a mark of the Christian disciple. The whole Church, all those who belonged to the Risen Jesus, is gathered together in one place. Mary, the mother of Jesus, is in the midst of the Church and shares in its prayer. Also present are "some women". Women have clearly played an important role in the ministry of Jesus according to Luke's Gospel (cf. *Luke* 8:1-3; 23:49; 23:55; 24:1-11) and they will have an important role in the life of the Church. They have been faithful to Jesus and now they are

---

70 Joseph A. Fitzmyer, S.J., "The Acts of the Apostles", Volume 31 of *The Anchor Bible series*, (New York: Doubleday, 1997), p. 5. © Yale University Press; reprinted with permission.

united to the eleven apostles (Judas having left them). The brothers of Jesus are mentioned once more. These are the close family of Jesus, and it is impossible to say for certain exactly what their relationship was. Jesus had made it clear that the members of his family were those who heard the word of God and kept it (*Luke* 8:21). The presence of these relatives is an important pointer to the fact that Jesus' close relatives became his disciples. Only the Eleven who had been specially chosen by Jesus, and Mary, his mother, are named. The others are mentioned but not named. She is described explicitly as his mother, so there is no possibility of mistaking who is being referred to. She is in the midst of those people who were closest to Jesus, and she has a special place among them. She alone is the mother of Jesus. According to what Luke says at the beginning of his Gospel, Mary welcomed in faith her task of giving the Messiah to the people of God, and she brought this task to fulfilment in a spirit of total availability and service. She had many things on which to reflect in her heart after the events at the beginning of the Gospel (cf. *Luke* 2:19, 51), and her soul was profoundly wounded as she shared in the rejection met by Jesus (cf. *Luke* 2:34).

At the centre of the newly-born Church is, of course, Jesus. All the others are present only because they have a close relationship with him. Mary belongs to their group, and she brings with her the unique relationship that she had with him. Each member of the Church strengthens the others, and they enrich each other in their relationship with Jesus.[71]

Reflect

Read again the text of *Acts* 1:13b-14.

Below are some questions that might help you engage with this text.

1. What do you think the group of disciples were praying about as they waited for the outpouring of the Holy Spirit?
2. What are you doing when you pray?
3. What place does Mary have in your prayer?
4. Are other people a distraction when you pray, or does their presence help you?

---

71 Klemens Stock, S.J., *Mary the Mother of the Lord in the New Testament*, (Rome: Edizioni Carmelitane, 2006), pp. 125-126.

Respond

This is the time for your heart to communicate directly with God. The prayer below might help you get started.

> *God our Father,*
> *you gave the Holy Spirit to your apostles*
> *as they joined in prayer with Mary, the mother of Jesus.*
> *By the help of her prayers*
> *keep us faithful in your service*
> *and let our words and actions be so inspired*
> *as to bring glory to your name.*[72]

Rest

The existentialist philosopher Jean-Paul Sartre famously said that "hell is other people". Diametrically opposed to this cynical outlook is the Christian worldview that speaks of the 'Kingdom' or 'Reign' of God, where peoples of every race, nation and way of life will be gathered together to live with God in eternal peace. The Eucharist is an essential aspect of the Christian life and "because there is one bread, we who are many are one body, for we all partake of the one bread" (*1 Corinthians* 10:17). We are also baptised into the one body of Christ (*1 Corinthians* 12:13).

In the text we have been considering, Mary is pictured with the other disciples waiting for the promise of the Holy Spirit. They were devoting themselves with one accord to prayer. This is the primitive Church. All are there because each had a personal relationship with Jesus, and he brings them together into the new family of God. The Christian life is not a lonely struggle to live by a high moral code; it is principally a relationship, the effects of which, of course, spill over into one's moral life. The relationship is with Jesus Christ, who is God Incarnate, and each relationship is unique. However, we cannot come into relationship with God in and through Jesus Christ without coming into relationship with people, and how we actually relate to others is the test of how healthy is the relationship with God.

Of course, there is an indispensable individual element to the spiritual journey. We are invited into a personal relationship with God, but this connection does not take us out of the world but plunges us more deeply into it. In the *First*

---

72 Alternative opening prayer for the Common of the Blessed Virgin Mary in the Easter Season, in *The Roman Missal* (London / Alcester: Collins / Goodliffe Neale, 1974).

Letter of John we are told: "Beloved, let us love one another, because love is from God; everyone who loves is born of God and knows God. Whoever does not love does not know God, for God is love." (*1 John* 4:7-8, *NRSV* translation). We cannot be content with a cosy relationship with God in which we receive comfort and protection from the "slings and arrows of outrageous fortune", as Shakespeare would put it. When we move deeper into the mystery of God, we encounter our neighbour, and this can be troublesome. Jesus made it very clear that loving one's neighbour was not to be separated from loving God (*Matthew* 22:34-40; *Mark* 12:28-31).

All of us have more in common than what separates us; we are united in the Source of life, from which we receive at each moment our existence. The spiritual journey leads inwards to find this Source in the centre of our own being, and at the same time, it leads outwards to recognise this same Source in others.

Act

You need the support of others on your journey, and others need your support. A kind word or even a smile can brighten up someone's life and lighten the burden that no one else is aware of. Praying for others is important, though if possible we should not confine ourselves to this but actively reach out with discretion where we are aware of a need. An important question to ask ourselves is whose needs are we attempting to respond to? Is it possible that helping others might just be for our own benefit? The 'false self' can insinuate itself anywhere!

Be aware of the other people in your world today. Pray for your fellow travellers, those with whom you live and work, the people you pass on the street. Each one is a beloved child of God.

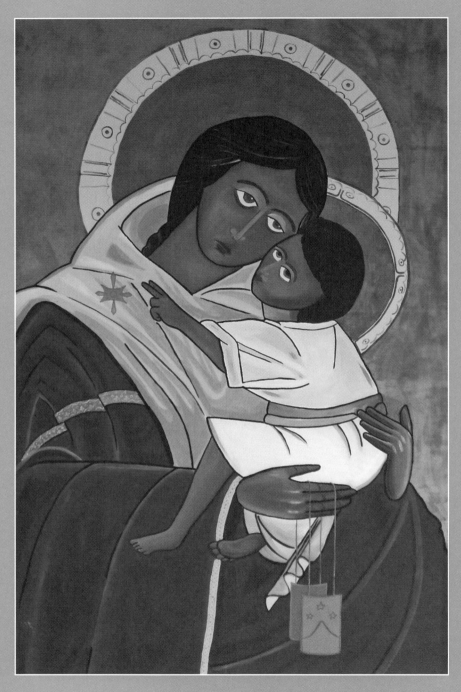

Our Lady of Mount Carmel
painting in the Carmelite-served parish of Calle Real, El Salvador.

THE MOTHER OF GOD'S OWN SON
Galatians 4:4-5

Opening Prayer

> *Loving God, in your Providence you chose the right time to send your Son as saviour of the world. You chose Mary to be his Mother, and his first disciple. Help me to listen to your Word and live by it each day. Through Christ Our Lord. Amen.*

Text

Read attentively the following Bible text for the first time in order to get an idea of the overall sense and to take in the details. This version, often called the *Knox translation* was first published in 1945 (New Testament) and in 1955 (New & Old Testaments together).[73] It was translated from the Vulgate Latin Bible, which is of course already a translation (by Saint Jerome). The *Knox translation* was used in Catholic circles for many years.

> [4] ... till the appointed time came. Then God sent out his Son on a mission to us. He took birth from a woman, took birth as a subject of the law, [5] so as to ransom those who were subject to the law, and make us sons by adoption.

Read

Saint Paul probably composed his letter to the Galatians between 53-55 A.D. In this brief text he lays out some essential elements of the Christian faith. Paul understands that God has a plan, and according to this plan the time had come to intervene decisively in human history. God sent the Son into the world and he took on human nature through an unnamed woman in order to set people free and give them the possibility of becoming children of God. The actual text says "that we might receive adoption", this is, that we might become members of God's own family. Jesus was a member of a particular people, and he participated in a human community. He was connected to a human and religious structure.

---

73 *The Holy Bible*, translated by Ronald Knox, (London: Burns & Oates, 1955).

Paul does not mention the name of Mary, but he emphasises her task. Mary's vocation was to be the mother of the Messiah, sent by God. Mary is the mother of God's own Son. It is through her that he has entered humanity and taken on all that it means to be human. This is the earliest New Testament allusion to Mary, the mother of Jesus.

Mary must respond to this divine decree. What characterises Mary above all is this task and this position that God has assigned her. God does not act without human cooperation. Mary has a special place in the divine plan of salvation; through her, God sends His Son into the world to lead to the fullness of life humanity that was subject to death.[74]

Reflect

Read again the text of *Galatians* 4:4-5.

God offers life to the world, but this is dependent on our co-operation. God sent his Son into the world, and – like all people – he was born of a woman. The relationship between mother and child is unrepeatable. The most important characteristic about Mary is precisely this unrepeatable task of being the mother of the saviour. We know from other parts of the New Testament that she accepted this role with joy, and continued faithfully to listen to the Word of God and live by it.

God is asking each one of us to be someone and to do something. We are to become the persons we have been created to be, and to do God's will for us. This, of course, is not always an easy task. However, if we take a wrong turning, God meets us on that road too, as we read in *Psalm* 139:

> [7] Where shall I go to escape your spirit? Where shall I flee from your presence? [8] If I scale the heavens you are there, if I lie flat in Sheol, there you are. [9] If I speed away on the wings of the dawn, if I dwell beyond the ocean, [10] even there your hand will be guiding me, your right hand holding me fast. [11] I will say, 'Let the darkness cover me, and the night wrap itself around me,' [12] even darkness to you is not dark, and night is as clear as the day.

(*Psalm* 139:7-12, *New Jerusalem Bible* version)

Perhaps you might reflect a little on your own call from God and your own faithfulness to it. The questions below are intended to assist this reflection.

---

74   See Klemens Stock, S.J., *Mary the Mother of the Lord in the New Testament*, pp. 130-31.

1. How do you fit into God's plan?
2. Can you recognise any wrong turns you have taken in your life?
3. Where was God at these times in your life?
4. What is required of you to be faithful to God's plan?

Respond

There is a time to think about God's place in your life, and a time to allow your heart to communicate directly with the One who has formed you in the womb (*Psalm* 139:13). The prayer below may help you.

> *Holy Mary, Mother of God,*
> *You have given the world its true light,*
> *Jesus, your Son – the Son of God.*
> *You abandoned yourself completely*
> *To God's call*
> *And thus became a wellspring*
> *Of the goodness which flows forth from him.*
> *Show us Jesus. Lead us to him,*
> *Teach us to know and love him*
> *So that we too can become*
> *Capable of true love*
> *And be fountains of living water*
> *In the midst of a thirsting world.*[75]

Rest

In the text we have been examining, Mary is not mentioned by name. The focus is on God who chose the right moment to send his Son into the world. It can be difficult to discern any divine plan in the mess that is our world. In this life we have to walk by faith, just as Mary did. Faith is the commitment to God who has revealed himself in the Scriptures, and above all in the life, death and resurrection of Christ. The Jewish people looked forward to the coming of the Messiah, but when he did come the majority could not accept him because he was not what they were expecting. Jesus was an unlikely Messiah. Even Paul persecuted the followers of Jesus, until the experience on the road to Damascus, when he too came to believe in the Lord. This was a profound shock for Paul, and it took him quite some time to put it all together in his own mind. His understanding of God's plan for the salvation of the world changed

---

75 Paragraph 42 of Pope Benedict XVI's 2005 encyclical, *Deus Caritas Est*, (available in various editions).

drastically because of his faith in Christ. He was probably a little bit advanced in his thinking, and he had little patience with those who could not keep up.

Some people see more clearly than others, but what matters in the end is that each of us respond wholeheartedly to whatever we believe God is asking of us. Saint Paul was an exceptional character; the rest of us have to be ever alert that the 'false self' (as described in reflection 8) does not insinuate itself into our faith. We may think that we see clearly, far more clearly even than the Church, but we should beware of following a personal opinion, especially if it is opposed to Christian teaching. The mystics often have a disconcerting way of expressing themselves, but they are aware that human language is a poor vehicle to describe what is beyond words. They are like poets who stretch the boundaries of language in a vain attempt to catch hold of an experience. The Gospels proclaim that Jesus is risen from the dead, but they do not try to describe the resurrection, which is beyond human words and human experience. Doctrines about God and morality can be put into words, but the encounter with God escapes definition. What can be judged are the external effects of this encounter.

We tend to be so preoccupied by our daily concerns that we are not aware of the bigger picture. God seeks in many ways to waken us up in order to share the divine life with us. God may use external events to do this, but God is not external to us. According to Saint John of the Cross, God is the centre of the soul,[76] its very substance,[77] the being of our being. In order to encounter God within, we must embark on the longest and most arduous journey we will ever take. It is difficult not because God wills it so, but due to the many obstacles that we ourselves place on our path. We are travelling from our own world that we know to another world that is completely new. Our 'false self' has nothing to cling onto because there is no security except the irresistible call from God who is beyond all knowledge. Our false self continually calls to us that this is a foolish venture, that it will end in disaster, that it is much better to return to the solid ground where it could exercise some control and gain some satisfaction. However, we have been created by God to share God's own life, and nothing less will ever fully satisfy us. We are continually impelled to slake the raging thirst within. Tragically, some seem to kill this desire and settle for so much less than their destiny. We who have heard the call will continue on the journey wherever it takes us.

Spend some quiet time now communing with God who calls you from within.

---

76 *Living Flame of Love*, I.12.
77 *Ibid.*, I.14.

Act

The false self will seek to railroad any attempt to take the spiritual journey seriously, because that threatens its pre-eminent place in your life. The false self can twist even prayer into a self-seeking occupation. Does our experience make us proud, judgemental or intolerant? Of course, the false self rushes to our defence immediately and vehemently denies any such possibility. However, in order to translate your prayer into your own life situation, you could step back and look at yourself, asking God's grace for this exercise. Is it possible that you are not quite as spiritually advanced as you hoped or thought? Do you reject those who tell you the truth? Listen today to everything that is said to you. Is it possible that God's message is hidden behind all the human words?

Mary, Queen of Heaven.
Window by Richard Joseph King at the
Church of Our Lady of Mount Carmel, Faversham, Kent, England.

REFLECTION 19

THE SIGN IN HEAVEN

Revelation 12:1-6

Opening Prayer

> *Dear God, you formed a people for yourself to be a light for the nations. From this people came forth the Messiah, your only Son. Protect all those who have faith in him. Help me to hear your Word, and let it be the guide of my life. Through Christ Our Lord. Amen.*

Text

Read attentively the following Scripture text for the first time in order to get an idea of the overall sense and to take in the details. The translation of our passage below is taken from the series *Sacra Pagina* which we used in reflection 13.[78] Each volume in the series is a translation and a commentary by one of the foremost Catholic biblical scholars.

> [1] A great sign appeared in heaven: a woman robed with the sun, with the moon under her feet, and on her head a crown of twelve stars. [2] She was with child, and she cried out in her pangs of birth, in anguish to be delivered. [3] Then a second sign appeared in heaven: a great red dragon with seven heads and ten horns and seven diadems on his heads, [4] and his tail swept down a third of the stars of heaven and hurled them to the earth. The dragon stood before the woman who was about to give birth, so that when her child was born he might devour it. [5] And she gave birth to a son, a male child, who is destined to rule all the nations with a rod of iron; but her child was snatched up to God and to his throne. [6] The woman fled into the desert, where she had a place prepared by God that there she might be sustained by God for twelve hundred and sixty days.

---

78 W. J. Harrington, 'Revelation', in *Sacra Pagina*, Volume 16, (ed.) D. J. Harrington, (Collegeville, Minnesota: Liturgical Press, 1993), p. 128.

Read

The Woman is the bride, the heavenly Jerusalem, the complete opposite of the harlot mentioned earlier in the *Book of Revelation*. The Woman is the people of God who give birth to the Messiah and the messianic age. The people of God become the Church and are taken into the desert for protection for a symbolic time. The Church must suffer before the final victory over evil.

It is no surprise that the Woman in this text has also been understood as Our Lady. Mary is not the primary figure intended in the text, but it is not stretching the text too far to see her also in it.

We misunderstand this kind of writing if we try to decodify it in order to know exactly what will happen at the end of time. The writer was trying to give courage to his fellow Christians who were most likely undergoing severe persecution for their belief in Jesus Christ. What is written speaks to our present situation just as much as our future.

There are many Old Testament allusions in our text. You might like to look up in your own Bible *Isaiah* chapter 60, verse 1, and then verses 19-21. This text speaks about the light that does or will surround the people of God. The *Song of Songs* (6:10) also gives some background. The image of the Woman giving birth has echoes in the Prophet *Micah* (4:10) and the Prophet *Isaiah* (66:6-10). Jesus himself used this idea of the Woman giving birth in the context of his passion (*John* 16:19-22). The Woman who cried out in the pangs of birth is not then a reference to Jesus' birth, but to the painful child-bearing of the new people of God, through the cross and resurrection.[79] However, the "son, a male child, who is destined to rule all the nations with a rod of iron" (verse 5) in our text is clearly the Messiah, Jesus. The rod of iron is a reference to *Psalm* 2. His birth, in this context, refers to his resurrection. His being "snatched up to God and to his throne" (verse 5) refers to his glorious ascension. The Woman fled into the desert, which is a highly symbolic place in the Old Testament. It is the privileged place of encounter with God.[80]

Perhaps you can see why some have seen Mary in the figure of the Woman in *Revelation* 12.

---

79 Ignace de la Potterie, *Mary in the Mystery of the Covenant,* (New York: Alba House, Society of St. Paul, 1992), p. 252.

80 For a *Lectio Divina* reflection on the figure of the prophet Elijah in the desert, see Joseph Chalmers, O.Carm., *The Sound of Silence: Listening to the Word of God with Elijah the Prophet,* (Faversham & Rome: Saint Albert's Press & Edizioni Carmelitane, 2007), pp. 97-109.

Reflect

Read again the text of *Revelation* 12:1-6.

The *Book of Revelation* or the *Apocalypse* is written in a style that is very foreign to most of us. It has often been used to try to describe exactly what will happen at the end of the world, without any thought for what the author intended. It is not a description of the 'End Times', but rather a rallying-cry to persecuted Christians, reminding them God would reward them greatly for their faithfulness.

Suffering is an unavoidable part of being human; some seem to suffer much more than others, but the shadow passes over every life at some time. When suffering, it is not easy to pray because our focus is naturally on ourselves and what we are experiencing. However, prayer should not be confined to a set time when we turn our attention specifically to God, but includes our whole life if we are fundamentally directed towards God. In this way we fulfil the exhortation of Saint Paul to "pray unceasingly" (*1 Thessalonians* 5:17), even when our attention is elsewhere. What is crucial is our intention, that is, the underlying motivation of our lives. When we love someone, he or she does not cease to be a vital part of our lives simply because we are focusing on something else. The love that we have is like an underground stream that emerges into the daylight from time to time. The fact that it cannot be seen at many points does not mean that it has ceased to exist; it flows on at a deeper level.

Does your relationship with God flow throughout the day, whatever you happen to be doing? The following questions are intended to help you reflect on what is the fundamental direction of your life.

1. What does prayer mean for you?
2. How do you express your relationship with God throughout the day?
3. How do you relate to God in good times and in bad times?
4. In the midst of suffering, how do you express hope in God?
5. What do you understand by having faith in God?

Respond

Let your heart now communicate with God. The modern translation of the psalm below may help.

> *My spirit soared when a Voice*
> *spoke to me:*
> *"Come, come to the Heart of Love!"*

How long I had stood within the house of fear
yearning to enter the gates of Love!

The New Jerusalem, the Holy City,
Is bound firmly together;
All who seek the Heart of Love,
Those who have faced their fears,
enter the gates in peace and with great joy,
singing songs of thanksgiving.
There, in harmony with the cosmos.
the community gathers united in love.

Pray for the peace of the world!
May all nations prosper as one!
May peace reign among all peoples,
and integrity dwell within every heart!
Then will friends and neighbors, and
former enemies as well,
cry out, "Peace be within you!"
For the good of the universe and
in gratitude to the Beloved,
Let us serve the Holy One
of all nations
with glad hearts.[81]

Rest

Although the *Book of Revelation* does not give details of what will happen at the end of the world, it does focus our attention on the fact that there is a struggle between those who seek good, and those who seek evil. God's triumph is assured, but those who follow the divine will cannot escape persecution in some form or another. In times of light, as in times of darkness, we are asked to hold on to faith. It is that relationship with God which will make sure our lives ultimately have meaning.

The trouble with faith is that it goes beyond the limits of human experience. Faith is absurd to those who do not admit of the possibility of anything beyond our limited human possibilities. Every day there are new discoveries, and exciting new possibilities open up to us. Communications have become much

---

81 A new version of *Psalm* 122 in Nan C. Merrill, *Psalms for Praying*, (New York & London: Continuum, 2002), p. 270.

easier in the recent past. We can keep contact with those we love on our mobile phone – "Hello, Mum, I'm on the train," – while sharing the vital news with the rest of the carriage. If we wish to keep our communications private, we could perhaps send a text message or an e-mail. Is there an end to human ingenuity? It is understandable that some people are so excited by human possibilities that they refuse to countenance any limits. However, God is not part of our created reality. God is completely Other, and cannot be accessed by our brilliant intellects. God gives us little sweets to attract us and, if we do not allow other things to crowd out the memory of these delicacies, we will become more and more attracted. The taste of these sweets is quite delicate, and it takes our palate a little while to really adjust. We can reject these little gifts from God and prefer courser food. The Israelites complained to Moses about what they had to eat in the desert, and they remembered the food they used to eat in Egypt (*Exodus* 16:1). The relationship with God has to develop gradually as our spiritual senses become more and more capable of receiving what God is offering to us.

God does not normally burst into our lives without warning and with the full panoply of divine attributes, because we would be incapable of handling the experience. God is Unconditional Love. An encounter with Unconditional Love inevitably reveals us to ourselves locked into the logic of self-preservation, which is the 'false self' system. If we try to understand God, we simply fit the Unknowable into what we already know, and therefore go astray. Of course, we can seek to understand what God has revealed, but in the relationship with God we can only leave behind all that we know and receive. Saint John of the Cross gives the image of leaving his house in darkness in order to go out to meet the One whom his heart loves:

> One dark night,
> Fired with love's urgent longings
> – Ah, the sheer grace! –
> I went out unseen,
> My house being now all stilled.[82]

When we move away from our own little world, where we are of course at the centre, we begin to be led into God's world. This is not an easy shift to make and disorients us completely because all our former points of reference are useless. By abandoning our own way of seeing and judging, we open ourselves to God's ways. This process of transformation normally takes a long time, as

---

82 *The Dark Night*, stanza 1.

the various layers of our being are made capable of being at home in this new world.

Take some time now in silence to invite God into your life and to continue the great work of transformation until you can see things no longer from your own narrow perspective but from God's.

Act

The 'false self' is mortally afraid of God because it is aware that the closer God comes, the less influence it can exercise, until finally it shrivels up. Really, the false self does not exist, as it is a figment of our imagination. It is made up of what we think of ourselves and how we want other people to think of us. However, the fact that it has no separate existence does not rob it of its power over us. We are much more than what appears on the surface, but we are normally dominated by false concerns. It is a long journey away from the ridiculous aspirations of the false self to the reality of who we are in God.

Perhaps today you could try to become aware of when your false self is operating. Why are you saying this or doing that? Are you seeking affirmation from other people? Is your judgement coloured in some way? When you see your false self in action, do not become angry with yourself but simply remember the presence of God that is always with you. Your glory is to be a child of God, no matter what other people may think of you.

*Window of Christ and Mary in the parish church and shrine
of Our Lady of Mount Carmel, Waterloo, New South Wales, Australia.*

THE WOMAN AND THE DRAGON
Revelation 12:13-18

Opening Prayer

Loving God, you desire to share your divine life with your creatures, and for this reason you have conceived a plan of salvation in Christ from the beginning of time. Protect from all dangers those you have chosen as your own. Help us to listen to your Word, and so be open to your love. Through Christ Our Lord. Amen.

Text

Read attentively the following Scripture text for the first time in order to get an idea of the overall sense and to take in the details. The version of the Bible used for this passage is a recent one, *New English Translation* (NET), made specifically to be put on the internet and accessed for free.[83] It is the work of some 25 biblical scholars and has a large number of notes by the translators so that readers can see why a particular word was chosen rather than another. The intention is that it can be regularly updated.

13 Now when the dragon realized that he had been thrown down to the earth, he pursued the woman who had given birth to the male child. 14 But the woman was given the two wings of a giant eagle so that she could fly out into the wilderness, to the place God prepared for her, where she is taken care of – away from the presence of the serpent – for a time, times, and half a time. 15 Then the serpent spouted water like a river out of his mouth after the woman in an attempt to sweep her away by a flood

16 but the earth came to her rescue; the ground opened up and swallowed the river that the dragon had spewed from his mouth. 17 So the dragon became enraged at the woman and went away to make war on the rest of her children, those who keep God's commandments and hold to the testimony about Jesus.

---

83 *New English Translation* (NET), (Bible Studies Press, 2005), available online at www.bible.org, copyright © 2006 Biblical Studies Press, reprinted with permission.

Read

The beast is allowed to wage war on the Church for a symbolic time, but it is always under God's special protection. Once again the principal meaning of "the woman" is the People of God, who have to undergo persecution in this life but can depend on the grace and protection of God. There is a long tradition which has seen Mary, the mother of Jesus, also in the figure of the symbolic Woman.

Satan cannot defeat the Woman and her offspring, no matter how hard he presses. The dragon is also called a serpent. This is a reference to *Genesis* 3, the prophecy that the serpent which tempted the first humans would have its head crushed by the heel of a woman. We have in our text an image of the direct attack against the people of God, the Church, which began at the beginning of time and will continue to the end. However, the victory of the forces of good is assured.

The figure of Mary is not the principal interpretation of the Woman but should not be totally excluded. Mary, the Mother of Jesus, is the personification of the Church in John's Gospel, which has some connections to the *Book of Revelation*. Remember also that Jesus calls her "Woman" in two pivotal scenes in John's Gospel (2:4; 19:25-27).

Reflect

Read again the text of *Revelation* 12:13-18.

Mary is the mother of the Church but also a member of it. What is your relationship to the Church? The following questions are intended to help you reflect on this important issue.

1. What is the Church?
2. What is your position with regard to the Church?
3. What can you do to build up the Church?
4. How can Our Lady build up the Church?

Respond

The following quote comes from the book of the prophet Zephaniah. Perhaps it might help you to respond to God from the heart, but what is really important is your own response.

Shout for joy, O daughter Zion! Sing joyfully, O Israel! Be glad and exult with all your heart, O daughter Jerusalem!

The LORD has removed the judgment against you, he has turned away your enemies; The King of Israel, the LORD, is in your midst, you have no further misfortune to fear.

On that day, it shall be said to Jerusalem: Fear not, O Zion, be not discouraged!

The LORD, your God, is in your midst, a mighty savior; He will rejoice over you with gladness, and renew you in his love, He will sing joyfully because of you,

as one sings at festivals. I will remove disaster from among you, so that none may recount your disgrace.

Yes, at that time I will deal with all who oppress you; I will save the lame, and assemble the outcasts; I will give them praise and renown in all the earth, when I bring about their restoration.

At that time I will bring you home, and at that time I will gather you; For I will give you renown and praise, among all the peoples of the earth, When I bring about your restoration before your very eyes, says the LORD.[84]

Rest

Some people seem to reject organised religion while claiming to maintain a close personal relationship with God in a private way. They stress that they can, and do, pray just as well at home as the hypocrites do when they go to church. There have always been hypocrites in the Church, and there always will be. In Saint Matthew's Gospel, we find the parable of the weeds among the wheat (*Matthew* 13:24-30). The workers sow good seed, but an enemy comes and introduces weeds, and when everything begins to grow it becomes clear that the beauty of the field is marred by the presence of the weeds. The workers want to uproot the weeds but the master will not hear of it because doing so at an early stage of growth could ruin the wheat, so he tells them to wait until harvest time. The desire of the workers is very understandable because the weeds certainly do take away from the appearance of the field of wheat. However, the master

---

84 *Zephaniah* 3:14-20. This text is from the *New American Bible* translation.

wants to give the wheat all the time necessary to grow properly. It is only at the end that weeds are pulled up and separated from the wheat.

Jesus wanted to describe the Kingdom (or the Reign) of God, and he did so in many ways including with the parable of the weeds among the wheat. The Church is not the Kingdom, but is preparing for it. Throughout the Scriptures we find the story of how God formed a people who would be his own possession among all the peoples of the Earth. From this Chosen People came the Messiah, through whose death and resurrection the way was open for the gentiles also to become members of God's Family. The Church is this Family of God, open to people from every race, language and way of life. The history of the Church is a well-publicised story of every kind of human failing side-by-side with a less well-known story of heroism and holiness. The Church seems to have the power to elicit very strong emotions, both for and against. Even those loyal sons and daughters of the Church can find themselves critical of some aspects of the organisation.

Wherever you find yourself within or outside the Church, following Christ is not a private, cosy relationship. Christ formed a group of disciples which was the nucleus of the Church after his resurrection from the dead. Coming into relationship with Christ inevitably brings you into relationship with other people. How you respond to these others – whether they are fellow believers or non-believers – will tell you a great deal about your relationship with God. In my own Carmelite tradition, the importance of solitude is stressed, but it is to be lived in a constant healthy tension with another value, that of community. In the Carmelite *Rule*, written originally for hermits in community, there is a movement from the solitude of the individual cell to the chapel at the centre where the community gathers. The community also gathers in the refectory where the body is fed as the spirit is nourished in the chapel. The solitary search for God in the cell gradually transforms the heart of the Carmelite so that when the community comes together, each has something of value to offer the group. Being together strengthens each individual to return to the cell in order to continue the search for God (or sometimes the struggle with God).

Spend some time in silence before God. Whether you are alone or in a group, God loves you passionately as an individual and desires to share the divine life with you. Open yourself to that love.

Act

The next time you go to church to join with other people, ask God to help you recognise the presence of Christ in them. The interaction with other people challenges our 'false self'. Look at your reactions to what people say and do. Are you annoyed because of some perceived slight? Do you preen yourself at the sound of praise? Do you seek attention and feel the need to deflect it from others?

The Church of Rome.
Ceramic by Adam Kossowski in St. Joseph's Chapel, Aylesford Priory, Kent, England.

SECTION SIX:

Mary in Later Tradition

The figure of Mary, the Mother of Jesus, has had a huge influence on the Church throughout the centuries. Christians have been divided, and still are, over her role in God's plan of salvation. Many artists have a fascination for her and it seems that every reputable art gallery throughout the world has several portraits of Mary, usually holding the child Jesus. It is impossible in a book of this size to do justice to the post-Scriptural development of thought about Our Lady. I simply want to reflect on two aspects of this development. The first is what she has meant for my own religious family, the Order of Carmelites, and the second is how I think she might speak to us in the early part of the twenty-first century.

The Carmelite tradition stretches back over 800 years and has many fascinating insights. The first relationship that Carmelites had with Mary was as their patroness. Along with all other Christians, they also understood that she was their mother, but the Carmelites also looked upon Mary as their sister, the one who walked side-by-side with them as they sought to remain faithful to Christ the Lord in all the ups and downs of life. In the reflection that follows I have picked out only one element of the very rich tapestry that displays the Carmelite relationship with Mary, often called by us "Our Lady of Mount Carmel", since the relationship began when the hermits on Mount Carmel dedicated their first chapel to her, whom they called "The Lady of the Place".

The final reflection, "Mary and Us", is intended to be a summing-up of all that has gone before. The Church has constantly reflected on the figure of Mary because she plays a significant role in the life of Jesus, and what we think of her can and does affect what we think of Jesus. At the end of the journey through the Scriptural texts, we meet a modern interpretation of her role. However, the most important thing in conclusion is what relationship each one of us has with Mary, the Mother of Jesus.

The icon of Mary as 'La Bruna' (the dark lady),
venerated in the Carmine (Carmelite friary) in Naples,
is probably the oldest surviving Carmelite image of the Blessed Virgin.

MARY AND CARMEL

Opening Prayer

Father, may the prayers of the Blessed Virgin Mary, Mother and Queen of Carmel, protect me and lead me more deeply into the mystery of your Word, who is Christ the Lord. Amen.

Text

On this occasion the text for our reflection is not from the Bible, but is instead an article from the *Constitutions* which express the spirituality and govern the internal workings of the Carmelite friars. From time-to-time throughout the centuries of the Carmelite Order's existence the *Constitutions* have been updated, the latest revision taking place in 1995.[85] The following is an adaptation of article 27:

Mary, overshadowed by the Spirit of God
gave a human face to the Word made flesh.
She is the Virgin of wise and contemplative listening
who kept and pondered in her heart
the events and the words of the Lord.
She is presented to us
as one able to read the great wonders
which God accomplished in her
for the salvation of the humble and of the poor.

Mary was not only the Mother of Our Lord;
she also became his perfect disciple, the woman of faith.

At the marriage feast in Cana, Mary taught us to believe in her Son;
at the foot of the Cross, she became Mother to all who believe;
with them she experiences the joy of the Resurrection.
United with the other disciples in constant prayer,

---

85 Available in Kevin Alban, O.Carm., (ed.), *Journeying with Carmel*, (Middle Park, Australia: Carmelite Communications, 1997). The *Constitutions* can also be found online via the Carmelites websites of the British Province (www.carmelite.org), the Australian Province (www.carmelites.org.au) and the Curia (www.ocarm.org).

she received the first gifts of the Spirit,
who filled the earliest Christian community with apostolic zeal.

Carmelites see in the Virgin Mary, Mother of God
and archetype of the Church,
the perfect image of all that they want and hope to be.
For this reason, Carmelites have always thought of Mary
as the Patron of the Order,
its Mother and Splendour;
she is constantly before their eyes and in their hearts
as the Virgin Most Pure.
Looking to her, and living in spiritual intimacy with her,
we learn to stand before God,
and with one another,
as the Lord's brothers.
Mary lives among us, as mother and sister,
attentive to our needs;
along with us she waits and hopes,
suffers and rejoices.

Read

An important element of Carmelite devotion to Our Lady is the 'brown scapular', two small pieces of cloth worn over the shoulders. The scapular devotion comes from a venerable tradition of the Order concerning an apparition of Mary to Saint Simon Stock, a medieval Carmelite friar. The scapular is a part of the Carmelite habit and adapted for everyday wear, especially by lay people. It is a reminder of Mary's commitment to us and our commitment to her. She is mother and sister, leading us and guiding us to Christ her Son in whom we find salvation. Pope John Paul II wrote in regard to the scapular: "It is a sign of the continual protection of the Most Holy Virgin, not only throughout life but also at the moment of the transition towards the fullness of eternal glory."[86]

Wearing the scapular is intended to be an outward reminder of what should be going on within. The danger with any outward sign is that it remains merely outward, and therefore the stress today is on the necessity of living what the scapular symbolises. Mary is seen to be the perfect example of what it means to follow Christ. The meaning of the scapular today can perhaps be summed up

---

86 Letter of Pope John Paul II, 25th March 2001, paragraph 5, available in Joseph Chalmers, O.Carm., *Mary the Contemplative*, (Rome: Edizioni Carmelitane, 2001), pp.85-88.

in one of the prayers over the people at the end of the Mass of the Solemnity of Our Lady of Mount Carmel: "Lord, grant that those who in devotion have put on the habit of Our Lady of Mount Carmel, may put on her virtues also and enjoy her unfailing protection".[87]

Reflect

I have shared a little of the Carmelite connection to Mary, the Mother of Jesus. You have your own relationship with her, and now is the time to reflect on that. I will suggest some questions to help you reflect on your own relationship with Mary, and what this means for your daily life.

1. What is your relationship with Mary? Does this relationship lead you close to God?
2. If you believe it is a close relationship, how does that show itself in your daily life? How do you imitate her virtues we find in the New Testament?
3. If you believe you have a very distant relationship with Mary, ponder on her example from the New Testament.
4. How does the example of Mary in the New Testament affect your treatment of other people?

Respond

Now is the moment to give free rein to your heart. Perhaps you want to address yourself to Mary, the Mother of the Lord, or to God in her company. The prayer below is intended to give you a kick start.

> *Rejoice, Mary, full of grace.*
> *Exult, Virgin of the pure heart,*
> *Because the Lord is with you.*
> *You are blessed among women,*
> *You are our mother,*
> *and our sister.*
> *Come and live with us,*
> *And pray for us to your Son Jesus.*[88]

---

87 *Carmelite Missal*, (Rome: Order of Carmelites & Order of Discalced Carmelites, 1979, revised 1997).
88 From a longer text by the Carmelite Fraternity of Pozzo di Gotto, Sicily, quoted in Emanuele Boaga, O.Carm., *The Lady of the Place: Mary in the History and in the Life of Carmel*, (Rome: Edizioni Carmelitane, 2001), pp. 200-205.

Rest

Mary was a contemplative, which does not mean that she spent all day on her knees. A contemplative is a mature friend of God who looks upon reality as if with the eyes of God and loves what she sees as if with God's heart.

After the stunning news that she received at the Annunciation, Our Lady hurried to visit Elizabeth who told her that she was blessed because of her faith. God does not require us to do very difficult things or great things. God wants to do great things in and through us. Mary co-operated with the Word of God, and so gave God space to work in her life. She was blessed not principally for what she did, but because of what God had done in her.

Mary listened to the Word of God; she pondered everything in her heart; she thought about what happened to her, and what was said to her, and she was able to discern the voice of God in the midst of her day-to-day reality. Like Mary, we are called to be contemplatives. We are called to contemplatively listen to the Word of God no matter how it comes to us. Our Lady had no barriers in her to the accomplishment of God's will. Therefore, she knew how to listen. We must learn how to listen. In order to be able to listen to God, we must be aware of our own hidden agenda. A hidden agenda is the collection of prejudices and ideas that really motivate much of what we do and say despite what we may believe to the contrary. These things are hidden very often from ourselves and sometimes from other people. At times what is motivating us is as clear as day to other people, while remaining hidden from ourselves.

God searches for men and women who will open their hearts and allow God to transform their lives, and through them to transform the life of the world. We must seek God's will by pondering the Word in our hearts as Mary did. So we must expect to be surprised by God. God will speak to us through the Scriptures, through the events of our day, and through the events within the society of which we are part. In order to hear the Word of God for us, we must seek to purify our own hidden agenda, which filters what God is saying so that we only hear what we want to hear.

We are asked to be faithful to God in our own particular situation. We are asked to live the Gospel where we are. We are asked to be contemplatives at the heart of the world, being aware of God's presence not in dramatic ways but in the midst of our ordinary everyday lives. Each of us then will be a focus for God's presence in our own little part of the world – rather like lightning conductors. We need to be aware of the presence of God within us and then in the people we meet. This awareness is not felt in any way but is an act of faith. God lives at the centre of each human-being no matter what that person is like. As we become more and more aware of God's presence everywhere, we become more sensitive to the signs of the presence of God's Kingdom.

Mary is our Sister, accompanying us on our journey of faith, sharing with us the joys and sorrows of life. She is our Mother, nurturing the life of God within us. She prays with us and for us that we may become mature friends of God.

Contemplation begins when we entrust ourselves to God, whatever way God chooses to come to us. However, we need to stay awake and recognise the approach of God who may come to us in totally unexpected ways. Mary received the Word of God through the message of an angel, but was also open to hearing God's voice at the foot of the cross. Elijah met God not in the earthquake or the fire or the mighty wind, but in the sound of sheer silence (*1 Kings* 19:11-13).[89]

If we accept God's invitation to begin this interior journey, we will of course meet with difficulties on the way because we will be brought face-to-face with ourselves. We will see ever more clearly the motives for our actions. We will see that sometimes even our best actions have selfish motives. This is very difficult to accept, and this is one reason why the spiritual journey is so difficult and why many might wish to turn back to a less challenging place. If, however, we but knew the gift God was offering us, we would continue our journey despite the painful revelations about ourselves which we were offered. On this journey we become less proud, less sure of our own virtue, but more reliant on the mercy of God and more aware that all human beings are our brothers and sisters.

Our world is undergoing great cultural upheaval as we begin the third millennium. There is a profound spiritual crisis in our times. What have we to say in this situation? The call to be contemplative is a vocation that affects the world. Contemplatives can be found in every walk of life. To be a contemplative is to respond in faith to a call from God who often seems to be hidden. In the midst of conflict and division, such people are tabernacles of God's presence, through whom God is powerfully present. Therefore, in the present situation of our world, we can use whatever skills we have been given for the good of others, but above all, we can respond to the still small voice that calls us into an intimate relationship with Jesus Christ, the only Son of the Father. This is

---

89   For a *Lectio Divina* reflection on Elijah's meeting with God on Horeb, see Joseph Chalmers, O.Carm., *The Sound of Silence: Listening to the Word of God with Elijah the Prophet*, (Faversham & Rome: Saint Albert's Press & Edizioni Carmelitane, 2007), pp. 103-109.

not a cosy intimacy, but through the relationship with God we will be gradually transformed to become what God knows we can be, and be totally available for the divine work in the world. Mary was totally available for God. She is our model, our Mother and our Sister, accompanying us and encouraging us to believe always in God's promises, especially when appearances seem most discouraging.[90]

ACT

As you go about your daily business, walk with Mary. She pondered on everything that happened and what was said in order to discern the will of God in her life. Ask her to help you do the same. What is God saying in your life? Listen to the still small voice of God in the midst of your daily activities.

---

90 These reflections are based on Chapter 6 of my book *Mary the Contemplative*, cited above.

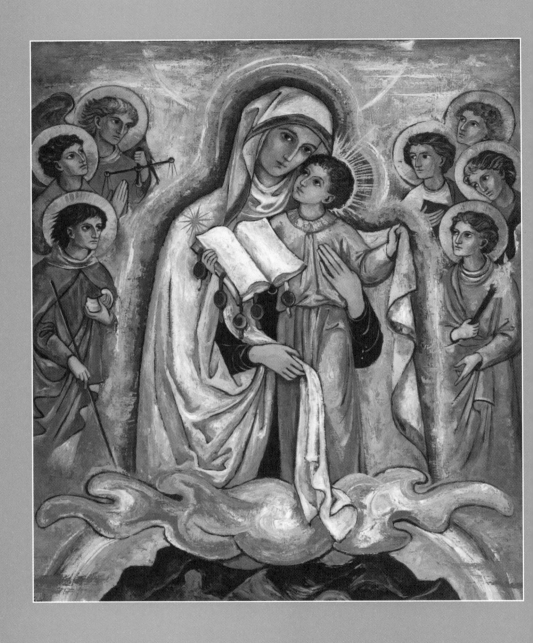

Our Lady of Mount Carmel with the infant Christ.
Painting by Roswitha Bitterlich-Brink (1954)
at CISA (Saint Albert's International Centre) in Rome, Italy.
It depicts Mary holding Christ, who himself holds open a book containing various seals,
representing the papal bulls granting privileges to the Carmelite Order.

MARY AND US

Opening Prayer

Loving God, you called Mary to be the Mother of your only Son and to follow him in faith. Help me to look to her as a model of how to listen to your Word and live by it. Through Christ Our Lord. Amen.

Text

Again the text in this reflection is not Biblical but is taken from one of the most important documents of the Catholic Church, *Lumen Gentium*, the 'Dogmatic Constitution on the Church', compiled during the Second Vatican Council in the mid-1960s.

> The sacred writings of the Old and New Testaments, as well as venerable tradition, show the role of the Mother of the Saviour in the plan of salvation in an ever clearer light and call our attention to it. The books of the Old Testament describe the history of salvation, by which the coming of Christ into the world was slowly prepared. The earliest documents, as they are read in the Church and are understood in the light of a further and full revelation, bring the figure of a woman, Mother of the Redeemer, into a gradually clearer light. Considered in this light, she is already prophetically foreshadowed in the promise of victory over the serpent which was given to our first parents after their fall into sin (cf. *Genesis* 3:15). Likewise she is the virgin who shall conceive and bear a son, whose name shall be called Emmanuel (cf. *Isaiah* 7:14; *Micah* 5:2-3; *Matthew* 1:22-23). She stands out among the poor and humble of the Lord, who confidently hope for and receive salvation from him. After a long period of waiting the times are fulfilled in her, the exalted Daughter of Sion, and the new plan of salvation is established, when the Son of God has taken human nature from her, that he might in the mysteries of his flesh free man from sin.

(*Lumen Gentium*, 55)[91]

---

91 Vatican II, *Dogmatic Constitution on the Church* (*Lumen Gentium*), 1964, in Austin Flannery, O.P., (ed.), *Vatican Collection*, Volume I, (Dublin: Dominican Publications, 1991), p. 415.

Read

The Second Vatican Council in the 1960s was a major event in the history of the Catholic Church. A number of important documents were issued, including the far-reaching Constitution on the Church, entitled in Latin *Lumen Gentium* ("Light of the Nations"). Before the Council there existed two divergent tendencies within the Catholic Church regarding the figure of Mary, and these led to a profound disagreement at the Council itself, which finally was resolved in a statement that claimed a large degree of agreement. A chapter on Our Lady was included in the document on the Church in order to bring out the relationship and to understand her role within the mystery of the Church and the community her Son established. The quote above stresses the prefigurement of the Mother of the Lord in the Old Testament.

In the wake of the Second Vatican Council a crisis arose within the Catholic Church regarding devotion to Mary. To encourage devotion, Pope Paul VI published a document – the 1974 Apostolic Exhortation *Marialis Cultus* – in which he stated that the Virgin Mary had always been proposed by the Church as an example to be imitated for the way in which she fully accepted the will of God. Saint Thérèse of Lisieux always had a close relationship with Mary, but she lamented the many sermons she listened to that stressed her glorious privileges and so put her on a pedestal out of the reach of ordinary people. Thérèse said that she wanted to hear about Mary's real life of faith.

Reflect

We have been through all the texts in the New Testament that touch upon the figure of Our Lady, and alluded to some of the Old Testament texts that by tradition have been taken to refer to her in some way. I have not tried to pull all these together into a coherent doctrine,[92] but perhaps at this stage you yourself might have built up a picture of her role in the Christian life in general, and in your life in particular. The following questions are intended to help you pull together some of the threads.

1. Why do you think there is no complete agreement in the whole of the New Testament regarding what Mary said and did?
2. What for you is the most important element emerging from the New Testament picture of Our Lady?

---

92 See the last section of Klemens Stock, S.J., *Mary the Mother of the Lord in the New Testament,* (Rome: Edizioni Carmelitane, 2006), entitled simply 'Mary, the Mother of the Lord'.

3. The Church has developed doctrines on Our Lady throughout the centuries, having meditated on the biblical sources. In the year 431 at the Council of Ephesus, she was declared to be *Theotokos* ("God-bearer" or "Mother of God"). What does this mean for you?
4. Jesus said to the beloved disciple from the cross, "Behold, your mother". What does this mean for you?

Respond

At the end of this journey of prayer with Mary, the Mother of the Lord, what does your heart want to say to God who called her to a very important task for the salvation of the world? God is calling you also. Perhaps the poem below might help to start off your heart-to-heart dialogue with God. It is taken from Chapter 2 of the *Song of Solomon*, often known as the *Canticle of Canticles*.

> [8] The voice of my beloved! Look, he comes, leaping upon the mountains, bounding over the hills. [9] My beloved is like a gazelle or a young stag. Look, there he stands behind our wall, gazing in at the windows, looking through the lattice. [10] My beloved speaks and says to me: "Arise, my love, my fair one, and come away; [11] for now the winter is past, the rain is over and gone. [12] The flowers appear on the earth; the time of singing has come, and the voice of the turtledove is heard in our land. [13] The fig tree puts forth its figs, and the vines are in blossom; they give forth fragrance. Arise, my love, my fair one, and come away. [14] O my dove, in the clefts of the rock, in the covert of the cliff, let me see your face, let me hear your voice; for your voice is sweet, and your face is lovely.[93]

Rest

The spiritual journey is essential in the process of finding out who we are, why we are here, and where we are going. The great philosophers of ancient times searched for wisdom and moved towards the light. The Judeo-Christian tradition firmly believes that God took the initiative to move towards us. God chose Abraham and made a covenant with him (*Genesis* 12:1-3). God promised that his descendents would be as many as the stars of heaven. Abraham and Sarah kept faith with God even when it was most difficult. God's mysterious messengers announced that they would have a son in their old age and it was through this child that God's promise would be fulfilled. Through the highs

---

93 *Song of Solomon* 2:8-14. This translation is taken from the *New Revised Standard Version*.

and lows of history God was faithful to the descendents of Abraham and Sarah. When they found themselves in slavery in Egypt, the God of Abraham, Isaac and Jacob called Moses to lead the people to the Promised Land. Moses wanted to know God's name and at the burning bush it was revealed: "I am who am" (*Exodus* 3:14). This is a mysterious name that perhaps hides more than it reveals. God is not part of our world but is outside our possibility of knowing. We can grasp that there is a God from the use of reason, but we can only know who God is because God chose to reveal the divine nature in many and various ways.

The people reached the Promised Land but they did not find their ultimate rest since they could not respond faithfully to the God who had made a covenant with their ancestors. Finally God decided to deal with this impasse definitively. The Chosen People could not be faithful, and so from them God raised up one who would be faithful unto death. "When the appointed time came, God sent his Son, born of a woman, born a subject of the Law, to redeem the subjects of the Law and to enable us to be adopted as sons." (*Galatians* 4,:4-5, in *The Jerusalem Bible* translation). This woman, Mary, the mother of Jesus, played an essential role in God's plan of salvation, but she had to journey by the light of faith as we all do. Her attitudes, as we discover them in the New Testament texts, can provide light for our journey and show us how to respond to the surprising ways of God.

On our journey there will inevitably be times of light and times of darkness. Mary has experienced these times and can help us to discern the will of God that is not always obvious. God has given Mary to us to help us on our journey. How we respond to God's gifts is an individual decision.

Act

The figure of Mary has often been a point of division among Christians. What do you believe about her role in God's plan of salvation? What kind of relationship do you have with her? What kind of relationship do you want to have? Ask her to help you understand what help she can offer you on your journey of faith. Listen throughout the day and watch as you respond to everything that happens to you. How do you think she would have responded? Is this telling you anything?

Our Lady blessing the scapular of Saint Simon Stock
Ceramic by Adam Kossowski on the Rosary Way at Aylesford Priory, Kent, England.

SELECT BIBLIOGRAPHY

There are innumerable books on the figure of Mary. Below is just a selection, which might be helpful to anyone who wants to go a bit deeper.

GENERAL RESOURCES ON MARY

Various contributors, *The New Interpreter's Bible*, (Nashville: Abingdon Press, 1995-2002). If you want to find out everything you ever wanted to know about the Bible, this 12 volume work is the place to go. The contributors are Catholic, Protestant and Jewish. The commentary is technical but there are also good pastoral reflections.

Raymond Edward Brown, Joseph A Fitzmyer, & and Karl Paul Donfried, *Mary in the New Testament*, (London: Geoffrey Chapman, 1978). This is the fruit of a discussion between Catholic and Protestant biblical scholars.

Sarah Jane Boss, (ed.), *Mary: The Complete Resource*, (London & New York: Continuum, 2007). This is a reference book on all aspects of Our Lady. It has an interesting chapter on Mary in the New Testament which seeks to outline some of the new ideas of Scripture scholars.

Raymond Edward Brown, *The Birth Of The Messiah* (London: Geoffrey Chapman, 1977). Everything you ever wanted to know about what the New Testament says regarding the birth of Jesus.

Daniel J. Harrington, (ed.), *Sacra Pagina* Series, (Collegeville, Minnesota: The Liturgical Press, 1991-). This is a 16 volume series on the New Testament by Catholic biblical scholars and is an excellent commentary. It is rather technical.

John Macquarrie, *Mary For All Christians*, (Edinburgh: T. & T. Clark, 1990, reprinted 2001). In this book, Professor Macquarrie studies the various doctrines concerning Mary and has a fine chapter on the New Testament evidence.

John McHugh, *The Mother of Jesus in the New Testament*, (London: Darton, Longman & Todd, 1975). This is a standard textbook on Mary in the New Testament.

Ignace de la Potterie, *Mary in the Mystery of the Covenant*, translated by Bertrand Buby, (New York: Alba House, Society of St. Paul), 1992. This is a rather technical book but it definitely repays study.

Klemens Stock, *Mary the Mother of the Lord in the New Testament*, (Rome: Edizioni Carmelitane, Rome, 2006). I mentioned this at the beginning as the work that inspired me to undertake the task of writing of this present work. This is short and simple, yet profound.

CARMELITE RESOURCES

If you are interested in following up reflection 21 on 'Mary and Carmel', the following may behelpful.

Kevin Alban, (ed.), *Journeying with Carmel*, (Middle Park, Australia: Carmelite Communications, 1997). This is a production of a part of the 1995 *Constitutions* of the Carmelite Friars, along with two very helpful articles.

Emanuele Boaga, *The Lady of the Place*, (Rome: Edizioni Carmelitane, 2001). This is a history of the Carmelite devotion to Our Lady up to modern times, with readings from significant Carmelite writers throughout the centuries.

Joseph Chalmers, *Mary the Contemplative*, (Rome: Edizioni Carmelitane, 2001). An examination of the Carmelite devotion to Mary, with emphasis on its connection to the core Carmelite value of contemplation.

Edmondo Coccia, (ed.), *In Communion with Mary: Our Heritage and Prospects for the Future*, (Rome: Edizioni Carmelitane, 2003). This book compiles the proceedings of the Carmelite Mariological Seminar held in 2001.

Christopher O'Donnell, *Loving Presence: Mary and Carmel*, Carmelite Spiritual Directory Series, (Melbourne: Carmelite Communications, 2000). This is a very fine study of the Marian heritage of the Order, but can be difficult to find copies of. It can be accessed online via the website of the Carmelite Curia: www.ocarm.org

Redemptus Valabek, *Mary Mother of Carmel*, 2 volumes, (Rome: Edizioni Carmelitane, 1987 & 1988). Two very popular volumes outlining the Carmelite devotion to Our Lady throughout the 8 centuries of the Order's existence.

John Welch, (ed.), *Carmel and Mary* (Washington, D.C.: The Carmelite Institute, 2002). A collection of articles on different aspects of Carmelite spirituality in relation to Mary.

MARY AND THE CHURCH

Michael Carroll, *Theotokos: A Theological Encyclopedia of the Blessed Virgin Mary*, (Dublin: Dominican Publications, 1982).

Austin Flannery, (ed.), 'Vatican Council II, Lumen Gentium: Dogmatic Constitution on the Church, 1964', in *Vatican Collection*, Volume I, (Dublin: Dominican Publications, 1991).

John Paul II, *Redemptoris Mater (Mother of the Redeemer)*, Encyclical Letter, 25th March 1987, (London: St. Paul Books & Media).

The Anglican-Roman Catholic International Commission (ARCIC), *Mary: Grace and Hope in Christ*, (Harrisburg & London: Morehouse, 2005). This is an agreed statement on Mary by the Commission established by Pope Paul VI and the Archbishop of Canterbury Michael Ramsey in 1967.

The [1992] Catechism of the Catholic Church (London: Geoffrey Chapman / Rome: Libreria Editrice Vaticana, 1994, and subsequent publishers), especially articles 484-511 & 963-75.

*This image of Our Lady of Mount Carmel is embossed in silver
to form the cover of a book (an edition of Laura Di Barezia's 'La Sposa Cristiana')
in the library of the Irish Province of Carmelites at Gort Muire, Ballinteer, Dublin.*

The Carmelite Family in Britain

The Carmelite Order is one of the ancient religious orders of the Roman Catholic Church. Known officially as the *Brothers of the Blessed Virgin Mary of Mount Carmel*, the Order developed from a group of hermits in thirteenth-century Israel-Palestine; priests and lay people living a contemplative life modelled on the prophet Elijah and the Virgin Mary. By the year 1214 the Carmelites had received a *Way of Life* from Saint Albert, the Latin Patriarch of Jerusalem.

Carmelites first came to Britain in 1242. The hermits became an order of mendicant friars following a General Chapter held in Aylesford, Kent, in 1247. Nuns, and lay men and women have always played a major part in the life of the Order, and have had formal participation since 1452. Over centuries of development and reform, the Carmelites have continued their distinctive mission of living 'in allegiance to Jesus Christ', by forming praying communities at the service of all God's people. The heart of the Carmelite vocation is contemplation, that is, openness to and friendship with God, pondering God's will in our lives.

Like the spirituality of all the major religious orders (Benedictines, Franciscans, Jesuits, etc.), Carmelite spirituality is a distinct preaching of the one Christian message. Carmelites blend a life of deep prayer with active service of those around them, and this apostolate takes many different forms depending on the time and the place Carmelites find themselves in.

Over the centuries 'Carmel' has produced some of the greatest Christian thinkers, mystics, and philosophers, such as Teresa of Jesus (of Avila), John of the Cross, and Thérèse of Lisieux (three Carmelite 'Doctors of the Church'). In the twentieth century, the Carmelite Family bore witness to the Gospel in the martyrdoms of Titus Brandsma, Edith Stein, and Isidore Bakanja.

England boasted the largest Carmelite Province in the Order until its suppression at the Reformation. The British Province was re-established under the patronage of Our Lady of the Assumption in the twentieth century. There are communities of friars, sisters and lay Carmelites across England, Scotland, and Wales. Similar communities exist in Ireland, and throughout the world. The international Order of Discalced (Teresian) Carmelite friars, nuns, and laity is also present in Britain and Ireland. Members of the Carmelite and Discalced Carmelite Orders work, live, and pray together to make up the wider 'Carmelite Family', which seeks the face of the Living God in parishes, retreat centres, prisons, university and hospital chaplaincies, workplaces, schools, publishing, research, justice and peace work, counselling, and through many other forms of ministry and presence.

Further sources of information on Carmelite spirituality include:

John Welch, O.Carm.
The Carmelite Way: An Ancient Path for Today's Pilgrim
(Leominster: Gracewing, 1996).

Wilfrid McGreal, O.Carm.
At the Fountain of Elijah: The Carmelite Tradition
(London: Darton, Longman and Todd, 1999).

Website of the British Province of Carmelites
www.carmelite.org

Carmel on the web

The British Province of Carmelites
www.carmelite.org

Aylesford Priory, Kent
www.thefriars.org.uk

National Shrine of Saint Jude, Faversham
www.stjudeshrine.org.uk

Lay Carmel in Britain
www.laycarmel.org

Corpus Christi Carmelite Sisters
www.corpuschristicarmelites.org

Discalced Carmelite Family in England, Scotland & Wales
www.carmelite.org.uk

Irish Province of Carmelites
www.carmelites.ie

Anglo-Irish Province of Discalced Carmelites
www.ocd.ie

Association of Discalced Carmelite Nuns in Great Britain
www.carmelnuns.org.uk

Carmelite Forum of Britain and Ireland
www.carmeliteforum.org

Carmelite Institute of Britain and Ireland
www.cibi.ie

International Carmelite Index
www.carmelites.info

The Carmelite General Curia
www.ocarm.org

CITOC – Carmelite Communications Office
www.carmelites.info/citoc

Carmelite N.G.O. at the United Nations
www.carmelites.info/ngo

Edizioni Carmelitane
www.carmelites.info/edizioni

Domus Carmelitana, Rome
www.domuscarmelitana.com

American Province of the Most Pure Heart of Mary
www.carmelnet.org

American Province of St. Elias
www.carmelites.com

Australian Province of Carmelites
www.carmelites.org.au

The O.Carm. – O.C.D web portal
www.ocarm-ocd.org

The Carmelite Institute of Britain & Ireland (CIBI)
offers distance-learning courses in Carmelite spirituality, history and culture.

CIBI was established in 2005 by the British Province of Carmelites, the Irish Province of Carmelites, and the Anglo-Irish Province of Discalced Carmelites.

The purpose of the Institute is to diffuse the charism, heritage and spirituality of 'Carmel' through part-time distance-learning courses in Carmelite Studies at introductory and more advanced levels.

The Institute's scholarly but accessible programmes are open to members of the Carmelite Family and anyone interested in the field of Carmelite Studies.

Through its interdisciplinary courses and activities the Institute offers an opportunity to learn about Carmelite life in its many forms, as well as a means to grow intellectually, spiritually and professionally.

CIBI's programmes – ranging from an *Adult Education Diploma* to a *Masters in Carmelite Studies* – are accredited by ecclesiastical and secular institutions of higher education, giving professional qualifications to those students who opt to submit assessments.

Thanks to the founders and sponsors of the Institute, programmes are made available to students at very reasonable rates, with a certain number of bursaries awarded to deserving individuals.

Though based in Britain and Ireland, CIBI enjoys close links with study institutes, libraries and heritage projects around the world, and welcomes student applications from any country.

For further information and a prospectus, please contact:

The Carmelite Institute of Britain & Ireland
Gort Muire Carmelite Centre, Ballinteer, Dublin 16, Ireland

☎ +353 (0)1 298 7706   Fax +353 (0)1 298 7714

E-mail: admin@cibi.ie

Website: www.cibi.ie

Also available by Joseph Chalmers

A Deeper Love (London & New York: Continuum, 1999) with Elizabeth Smith.

In Allegiance to Jesus Christ: Ten Conferences on Carmelite Life,
(Rome: Edizioni Carmelitane, 1999, reprinted 2004).

Mary the Contemplative, (Rome: Edizioni Carmelitane, 2001, reprinted 2004 & 2007).

*In obsequio Jesu Christi: The Letters of the Superiors General O.Carm. and O.C.D.
1992-2002*, (Rome: Edizioni OCD, 2003), with John Malley & Camilo Macisse.

The Sound of Silence, (Faversham & Rome: Saint Albert's Press
& Edizioni Carmelitane, 2007).

Carmel – School of Prayer, (Rome: Edizioni Carmelitane, 2010).

Also available in the
Carmelite Bible Meditations series

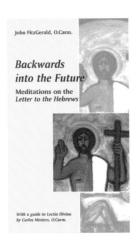

John FitzGerald, O.Carm.
*Backwards into the Future:
Meditations on the Letter to the
Hebrews*

Joseph Chalmers, O.Carm.
*The Sound of Silence:
Listening to the Word of God
with Elijah the Prophet*

Johan Bergström-Allen, T.O.C. &
Wilfrid McGreal, O.Carm. (eds.)
*The Gospel Sustains Me: The Word
of God in the life and love of
Saint Thérèse of Lisieux*

These and other titles on Carmelite spirituality
and history can be ordered from:

The Friars Bookshop
The Friars
Aylesford
Kent
ME20 7BX
United Kingdom

☎ + 44 (0)1622 715770

E-mail:
bookshop@thefriars.org.uk

Saint Albert's Press
Book Distribution
Carmelite Friars
P.O. Box 140
ME20 7SJ
United Kingdom

☎ + 44 (0)1795 537038

E-mail:
saintalbertspress@carmelites.org.uk

Edizioni Carmelitane
Via Sforza Pallavicini, 10
00193 Roma
Italy

E-mail:
edizioni@ocarm.org

Saint Albert's Press
www.carmelite.org/sap

Edizioni Carmelitane
www.carmelites.info/edizioni

LAUS DEO SEMPER ET MARIAE